Presented To:

_____

From:

_____

Date:

_____

# TAKE YOUR FREE
# PRODUCTIVITY ASSESSMENT

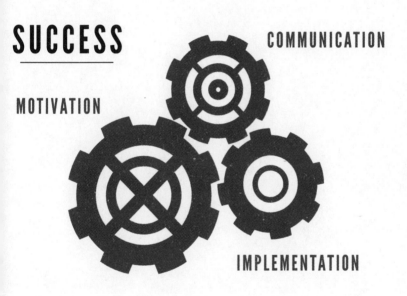

SUCCESS

MOTIVATION

COMMUNICATION

IMPLEMENTATION

Visit
**WWW.ULTIMATEPRODUCTIVITY.COM**
& Use Promo Code: 586404

# THE ART OF
# PRODUCTIVITY

YOUR **COMPETITIVE** EDGE

## JIM STOVALL

TO CLAIM YOUR ADDITIONAL FREE RESOURCES
PLEASE VISIT soundwisdom.com/jimstovallbooks/

SOUND WISDOM
P.O. Box 310
Shippensburg, PA 17257-0310

For more information on publishing and distribution rights, call 717-530-2122 or info@soundwisdom.com

Quantity Sales. Special discounts are available on quantity purchases by corporations, associations, and others. For details, contact the Sales Department at Sound Wisdom.

While efforts have been made to verify information contained in this publication, neither the author nor the publisher assumes any responsibility for errors, inaccuracies, or omissions.

While this publication is chock-full of useful, practical information, it is not intended to be legal or accounting advice. All readers are advised to seek competent lawyers and accountants to follow laws and regulations that may apply to specific situations.

The reader of this publication assumes responsibility for the use of the information. The author and publisher assume no responsibility or liability whatsoever on the behalf of the reader of this publication.

ISBN 13 HC: 978-1-937879-54-9
ISBN 13 TP: 978-1-937879-72-3
ISBN 13 Ebook: 978-1-937879-55-6

For Worldwide Distribution, Printed in the U.S.A.
1 2 3 4 5 6 7 8 / 20 19 18 17

Cover/Jacket design by Eileen Rockwell
Interior design by Terry Clifton

# DEDICATION

This book is dedicated to the memory of my mentor and friend Coach John Wooden. As a champion and as a leader, he taught me that a productive life is a successful life, and a successful life is a productive life.

It is also dedicated to my corporate family at the Narrative Television Network whose productivity makes the world a better place.

# CONTENTS

# FOREWORD

*by Steve Forbes*

I became aware of Jim Stovall in the late 1990s when we at Forbes were compiling a book that was subsequently released in 2000 entitled *Forbes Great Success Stories: Twelve Tales of Victory Wrested from Defeat.* That book contained Jim Stovall's story along with those of Donald Trump, Tom Monaghan, and others whose real-life adventures in capitalism point out what makes our system the best in the world.

I was then proud to endorse Jim's book *The Ultimate Gift,* which, at this writing, has sold 4 million copies around the world and has been made into a major motion picture from 20<sup>th</sup> Century Fox starring James Garner, Brian Dennehy, and Abigail Breslin. There have been three other books in *The Ultimate Gift* series, and *The Ultimate Life* starring Peter Fonda and *The Ultimate Legacy* starring Raquel Welch completed the film trilogy.

I have been quoted as calling Jim Stovall one of the greatest men of our era—not solely for the things he has done, but for the fact that Jim Stovall has dissected his own success and put it on display for others to follow through his speeches, newspaper columns, and books such as the one you hold now.

In *The Art of Productivity*, Jim Stovall strikes at the heart of success and failure for all of us individually and as a society. Natural and human resources abound, but how we harness them to create our own personal success is determined by our ingenuity and productivity. In this book, you will learn how to maximize your own productivity by discovering and releasing your core strengths in the critical areas of motivation, communication, and implementation.

I believe if we will let Jim Stovall lead us through our own Art of Productivity and Ultimate Productivity Profile, we will all become better people and grow closer to our potential. In the final analysis, we cannot be judged in comparison to anyone or anything but only in the reflection of our individualized mirror that reveals our potential.

Steve Forbes

## CHAPTER ONE

# THE ART OF BEGINNING

In our society, we tend to separate all endeavors into either art or science. While art is creative, it also contains elements of science through balance, form, and perspective. Science—while being very organized and regulated—contains artistic elements of creativity and expression. In this book, you will begin to see productivity toward your goals from both perspectives.

I am grateful to you and everyone who takes the time, effort, and energy to buy and read one of my books. By virtue of the fact that you selected this book, I assume that there are aspects of your life you would like to change, develop, or improve. If this is the case, read on. If this is not the case and you are truly satisfied with every area of your personal and professional life, stop reading this book immediately and go get your money refunded that you spent to purchase this book.

This may be the third book you have read this month or, on the other hand, it might be the first book you have read since high school. I have had an interesting relationship with books throughout my life. For the first three decades of my life, I don't know that I ever read an entire book cover to cover. I got through high school and even college by reading as little as necessary to matriculate through the process.

This seems ironic to me today, because when I had my eyesight and could read the words on a page as you are doing now, I never did it. Then, at age 29, I began my life as a totally blind person, and from that day to this one—thanks to audiobooks from the Library for the Blind and a high-speed digital player—I have actually read a book every day.

When you go 30 years completing a full-length book each day, you form a unique relationship with books. They have become a major part of my life. I read books for entertainment. I read books for information. And after reading many thousands of books, I can state with certainty I have read a handful of books for transformation. These books have impacted me so deeply that they have changed who I am and how I live my life. My fervent hope is that this book will be that kind of transformational experience for you.

Within these pages, you will have the opportunity to define your own success, create a life mission to achieve success, forge productivity on your own terms, and then begin to succeed by effectively utilizing motivation, communication, and implementation.

As an author, columnist, and speaker in the field of personal development, I have been exposed to many success systems, theories, and philosophies. They all have a certain degree of validity. But I feel, in many ways, the current state-of-the-art in the field of success and achievement is lacking a critical component.

There are many books or systems that will teach you to set a goal, create milestones, pursue your passion, and make changes in your world. These are important steps, but unless you have the practical tools to achieve and succeed at your fingertips, you don't have a chance.

Let's assume that I wanted to be a champion golfer. I could have this firmly established in my mind as a goal, pursue it with passion, and exhibit the highest degree of determination; but without practical, realistic instruction, I would be doomed to failure, even if I sought advice from the best golfer in the world. If, indeed, the legendary champion Jack Nicklaus himself gave me lessons, I wouldn't have a chance unless his instructions were mechanically sound and specific to me.

If Mr. Nicklaus simply told me to hit the ball farther than anyone else straight down the fairway and never forget to make every putt inside of 20 feet and then left me to my own devices, my game would never improve, and my goal of being a champion golfer would go to my grave with me just as most people's passions, desires, and goals go to their graves with them. However, if my instruction included mastering motivation, communication, and implementation as you are going to discover through *The Art of Productivity*, I would have the opportunity to succeed as a golfer.

Before you learn to master and apply these principles, it is vital for you to decide what changes you want to bring into your life. In order to make this kind of decision, you first need to establish where you are today and take full responsibility for your current state in every area of your life. Only when you accept the responsibility for your past that has resulted in your current condition can you then take control of your actions today, which will create your future success tomorrow.

We live in a society full of people who love to blame their mediocrity on everyone and everything other than themselves. As a corporate and arena speaker, I have had the privilege of talking with literally millions of people. After some of these events, I have a chance to visit with people who have sat in my audience. Oftentimes, these people share with me that their life is not where they want it to be; they are not pursuing their passions, nor reaching their goals, but they invariably hasten to add, "If you knew my family, you would know why I'm not succeeding." Or, "I'm where I am today because my boss is an idiot, and the weather's too hot, and the taxes are too high, and besides that, Jim, I'm a middle child."

When it comes to failure, one excuse is about as good as another. In fact, the next time your life is not turning out the way you want it to be, don't blame anyone else, just use my world-famous Jim Stovall, one-size-fits-all, 100 percent money-back guaranteed excuse for all situations.

Here is how it works. Instead of blaming everyone and everything around you for your condition, simply locate the nearest mirror, look directly into it, and say the magic words: "I guess I really didn't want it that badly."

This will work for you every time because unless or until you accept responsibility for the choices you have made in the past that have brought you to this place, you can never take control of your future. Now, I can imagine you thinking that I don't understand your situation, your background, and the barriers you face. This is true, and as a blind person myself I certainly realize that bad things can happen to good people, but for every person you can show me who has been defeated by a given circumstance, I will show you someone else facing that same circumstance who has used it as a springboard to do greater and more significant things in their lives.

Before you determine where you want to go in the world, there is one critical navigational element. You must first establish exactly where you are. Maps, directions, and even global positioning devices can only help you reach your destination if your current position has been established.

If you want to be wealthy before you decide what wealthy means to you, you'd better establish your current financial position. If you want to lose weight, you've got to get on the scales today. If you want to create the lifestyle of your dreams in every area of your personal and professional existence, you've got to be totally honest with yourself and elicit the honest opinions of those around you.

This honest assessment is a difficult process because we have a tendency to judge everyone else's performance while judging our own intentions. It's easy for us to smugly assert, without reservation, that the other guy was inexcusably late for his appointment. But when we find ourselves running behind schedule, we somehow come to the conclusion that we weren't late. It was simply that we missed every traffic light; we had to stop for gas; and who knew that there would be a traffic jam, a detour, and road construction en route to our destination?

If you're going to live the life of your dreams through the Art of Productivity by mastering motivation, communication, and implementation, you're going to have to be totally honest with yourself about where you are. The most destructive lies we ever tell are those lies we tell ourselves, because after a while we start to believe these falsehoods and begin sharing them with the world as if they were true.

One of my favorite actors, Jack Nicholson, in one of his best movies convincingly created a character who uttered the famous words, "You can't handle the truth." While it's not easy and never fun, I want you to know you can handle the truth, and it will be your first step toward making your life everything you want it to be.

As you accept responsibility for where you are and the choices you have made, you will begin to discover that while you have made some bad choices, in many cases you are mired in mediocrity because you have made no choice at all. I believe that in this world there are a few people who make good choices, and they enjoy every reward they seek. There are a few people who make bad choices, and they live in places like Leavenworth and San Quentin. But then there are the vast majority of people who make neither good nor bad choices; instead, they make no choice at all. These are the people who neither make things happen nor even watch things happen. They simply don't realize that anything happened.

I am reminded of a story about Irish emigrants coming to the United States during the earliest part of the 20th century. One particular family saved for many years to get the passage for the mother, the father, and three children. Even with all of their effort and diligence in saving their money, they were only able to purchase a ticket in what was known as steerage. This was a small, cramped area below deck where they had to sleep and pass the many days of the transatlantic voyage.

The family had brought some bread, cheese, and water with them to sustain them through the journey, but they rapidly consumed all of their rations with many days left in the voyage. From their squalid quarters below deck, they could see through the cracks between the planking onto the main deck above them. They observed first-class passengers dressed in all of their finery devouring a sumptuous banquet just a few feet away from where they were literally starving.

Finally, in desperation, the father crawled down the passageway and stepped up onto the main deck, and asked one of the stewards if he could have a few scraps or leftovers, lest his family starve to death below deck. The shocked steward replied, "Sir, this banquet is provided three times daily for all of our passengers. You and your family have been starving when you could have been feasting on the very best all along."

Before you launch into your quest to make your life everything you want it to be through the Art of

Productivity, be sure you have set your sights high enough. A person who doesn't make a choice is no better off than a person who doesn't have a choice at all; but a person who accepts less than their true destiny is relegated to a life of mediocrity. When you have seen yourself in your mind's eye on top of the world, anything less will leave you wanting.

We have all had dreams and secret passions inside of us for many years. When we were teenagers or young adults, the world seemed pregnant with possibility. But somewhere between there and here, this thing we call reality set in, and we got so busy making a living that we forgot to create a life.

Your destiny awaits.

## CHAPTER TWO

# THE ART OF DEFINING SUCCESS

There are very few times in life when being selfish or self-centered is desirable; however, when you're setting your goals, it needs to be all about you and what you want to be, do, or have.

Whether you're reading my book or anyone else's that purports to guide you to success, you first need to agree on a definition of success and be sure the person leading you knows how to get there.

All of my grandparents and both of my parents come from a pleasant town called Springfield. Springfield has much to recommend it in the way of historical sites and recreational activities. Let's say you and I agree to meet for a long weekend in Springfield to discuss our respective professional and personal goals as well as enjoy some of the local attractions and recreational activities.

This sounds like a pleasant prospect to me, as I hope it would to you; however, unless you were acquainted with my grandparents or parents, you and I would have a tremendous challenge getting together because there are over 30 cities and towns in the United States named Springfield.

I'm sure many of the various Springfields have wonderful attractions and notable attributes; however, unless we agree on the same Springfield, we will not get together, and my directions and roadmap will be useless to you.

In each of the more than 30 Springfields across the country, there are people who were born and raised there or have chosen it as the best place for them and their families to live their lives. Millions of people call Springfield home, but they do not mean the same thing when they use the word *Springfield* or *home*.

Success is much the same. I am convinced that there are as many definitions for success as there are people. More people fail, not because they are unable to reach their goal, but instead, because they have defined their goal or success as the wrong thing.

Success is probably the most private and personal definition you and I will ever establish; therefore, as we work toward creating our own picture of success, we can only accept limited help along the way. If this weren't difficult enough, the challenge of defining success is compounded when you realize that your personal success definition will be constantly changing throughout your life.

Many self-proclaimed success gurus encourage us to compartmentalize our success. They may label these compartments financial success, business success, family success, fitness success, etc. While I would agree these are all components of your personal success definition, you can't truly succeed in one area while failing miserably in another.

The Titanic, which had been called unsinkable as it was being built and launched, became the most famous ship of all time for doing the one thing no one wants their ship to do—that is, to sink. There might be many definitions of a successful ship—whether it be militarily, financially, aesthetically, or in overall performance—but I think we can all agree, in ship terms, sinking could be synonymous with failure.

When the Titanic was constructed, it was built with a number of watertight compartments. The engineers designed the Titanic to stay afloat even if several of these compartments were flooded. Unfortunately, all of the compartments were connected at the top, so when the Titanic hit an iceberg in the North Atlantic, the water that flooded several of the compartments overflowed at the top and flooded the entire ship; therefore, the Titanic sank.

Your and my success is much the same way. Failure in any area will affect all areas.

Success could be looked upon like a three-legged stool. For the sake of this analogy, you might have a financial success leg, a family success leg, and a physical success leg. It is important to realize that you can become the greatest financial success the world has ever known, but if you lose your family and ruin your health in the process, you will not be successful, even if the world may view you as a success.

Our media-driven society has created a phenomenon over the past several decades that is unique to our modern culture. Through magazines, television, radio, the Internet, and every other means of communication, we are bombarded with information about people and how they live. People have become famous in ways they never were before. We have always admired famous athletes, but now we may know where they spend their vacation, what they like to eat for breakfast, and the name of their dog.

People have always admired great artists and actors, but now we know every sordid detail of not only their professional lives, but we know far more than we need to about their personal lives. We constantly consume information and images about the lifestyles of the rich and famous and how some people are rising to the pinnacle of our society while others are falling from that same pinnacle and plummeting toward the depths of disgrace.

In this environment, it is easy to get a warped view of success. One of the big lies we are bombarded with regularly is the corrupting thought that if we had enough money, all our problems would be solved. One need look no further than the daily headlines to learn about some of the wealthiest among us who have lost their health, sacrificed their family, disregarded their integrity, and have subjected themselves to all manner of human failure.

Recent studies of people around the world from the wealthiest to those living in abject poverty reveal that beyond the basic necessities of food, clothing, and shelter, more money doesn't make us happy and, therefore, successful.

Any discussion of money and success would be lacking if I did not state that money is neither good nor bad. In the hands of good people, money can build places of healing, worship, and learning. In the hands of bad people, money can create death, disease, and destruction. In my life, I have been very poor and very rich. All other things being equal, never forget that rich is better.

While money, in and of itself, will not create success, I believe from my personal and professional contact that Bill Gates, Warren Buffett, and Steve Forbes are each, in their own way, quite successful. They are not a success because they have amassed great wealth; instead, they are successful because they have created value in the lives of other people that has brought them wealth, and they have utilized their financial success to make the world a better place. If money were a prerequisite to being successful, we would all have to agree that Mother Teresa was an absolute failure.

Fame and notoriety have been mistakenly labeled as success by many in our society. We have people whose names have become household words for playing baseball, being on a television show, eating insects on an island, dating a famous person, and there are even people today who are famous for nothing more than being famous. As a society, we have all gotten caught up in a massive parade, and no one has yet stopped to take a deep breath and consider the fact that we're not following this person because they're famous. Instead, this person is famous because we're following them.

Fame, in and of itself, is not a factor in success. Some of the most famous people in the 20th century would include Winston Churchill, Franklin Roosevelt, Adolf Hitler, John F. Kennedy, Sandra Day O'Connor, Martin Luther King Jr., and Lee Harvey Oswald. Some of these people, we would all agree, lived lives of great success while others were miserable failures in spite of their fame.

Some of the most successful people in the world will never be known by anyone other than the people whose lives they powerfully and positively impact. These people have defined success in such a manner that achieving their life goals does not bring them fame and notoriety. In some cases, their anonymity is a byproduct of their success goal, and in other cases they have defined success, at least partially, as living their lives away from the spotlight.

Success has, furthermore, been misdefined as being young, healthy, or beautiful. While these are all desirable traits in the right time and place, they are not a sole determinant of what we would call success. Those who worship at the altar of youth and beauty will necessarily find themselves fighting a losing battle. Your hairdresser, tailor, and plastic surgeon can only do so much. If you define yourself, totally, by the image in the mirror, if you simply live long enough, you will fail due to your own misguided definition of success.

While you will have to fill in the details and the specific elements of your own success, when it's all said and done, you will find that success comes when you live a life of productivity on a mission toward a worthwhile goal that brings you happiness, passion, and fulfillment.

## CHAPTER THREE

# THE ART OF ESTABLISHING A MISSION

Every few years, a new hot topic emerges among business writers, speakers, and consultants. These people are constantly on a quest to reinvent the wheel or, at least, reinvent new books, speeches, and consulting contracts. The same things that made people successful in the 19th century will bring you success in the 21st century.

Success is simple, but the mission toward success is never easy if you have established a worthwhile, significant, and meaningful goal. If you are a mountain climber, it might be your goal to climb Mt. Everest. If this is the case, you have now established a goal and defined success in your own terms. This is the simple part. Your mission is what you will find to be the not-so-easy part.

With tremendous preparation, sacrifice, and effort, you're going to have to start at the bottom of Mt. Everest and make your way to the top; therefore, success is a destination even if it's a moving target while your mission is that ongoing, constant journey toward success.

Several years ago in corporate America, it became trendy for each organization to establish a mission statement. I don't mean to diminish the validity of having and maintaining a corporate mission statement. Very few organizations have a mission statement that is really valid and meaningful to the people tasked with creating success. Unless their corporate mission statement is carved in granite on the outside of their building or suspended in gold leaf in the reception area, most employees don't know there is a mission statement, much less what it might be.

There is a fundamental disconnect between most organizations and their established mission statement. If you came into that organization as a cold outside observer and simply watched the collective activity day after day, it would be difficult to discern their mission statement.

The engraved platitude memorialized in stone outside corporate headquarters may say, "We exist to provide the best products and services for each and every one of our customers and, in doing so, we endeavor to improve their lives and create peace on earth and good will toward men." If you observe the average employee, you might surmise their mission statement to be, "We come to work as late as we can, do as little as possible, avoid interaction with executives and customers so as to continue receiving a paycheck and benefits as long as humanly possible."

Employees within an organization whose actions express this sentiment are not pursuing their own goal; instead, they have found themselves on someone else's mission for which they feel no passion, energy, or commitment. This does not necessarily make them bad people. It makes them misguided souls wandering through a world of limitless opportunity and possibility in which they are not engaged.

As important as it may be for organizations to have a mission statement that is truly meaningful to all concerned, it is even more important that you and I have a personal mission statement that defines our personal and professional journey toward our own definition of success.

I have had a personal mission statement of this kind for several years. I would like to tell you that I created it by myself but, in reality, my personal mission statement was given to me secondhand from my grandmother.

My grandmother played a vital role at several critical points in my life. When I was very young, I had a sister who was a couple of years older than me. She became very ill with what was later diagnosed as a form of leukemia. If you have seen *The Ultimate Gift* movie based on my novel of the same title, you will remember the young girl suffering with leukemia who was played by Abigail Breslin. Many elements of that character were based upon my sister. Due to her illness and my parents' subsequent travels taking her from hospital to hospital and specialist to specialist across the country, I spent a lot of time with my grandparents as a very young child.

Some of my earliest memories are of my grandparents and learning valuable lessons from people who had gone through a depression, a world war, and the building of what we know as the modern world. Tom Brokaw labeled these individuals collectively as the Greatest Generation. While I agree with Mr. Brokaw's assessment, I don't believe that generation was created with any more greatness than we have been created with. They simply were confronted with circumstances that required great people.

Several years later as a teenager, I was diagnosed with a very serious eye disease that would eventually rob me of my sight. In that time of adjustment from being fully sighted to partially sighted and then moving into blindness, I remember my grandmother being a tremendous support and encouragement. Through her words and deeds, she taught me the difference between sight and vision.

I learned that sight is the ability to see the world around you by capturing images through your eyes into your mind. Vision is the ability to capture the world around you in your mind as it should be and make it a reality. Both sight and vision are valuable commodities, but as a person who has lived with and without both, given the choice I would prefer vision to sight.

In my twenties, I spent some time as a Wall Street investment broker and then, as a totally blind person, launched a company called the Narrative Television Network, which makes movies, television, and educational programming accessible to 13 million blind and visually impaired Americans and many millions more around the world. Through that process of building a successful company and being recognized at the White House as the Entrepreneur of the Year and then recognized by the U.S. Chamber of Commerce as the Businessperson of the Year, I began receiving invitations to speak at corporate and arena events across the country.

Somehow, as happens to all of us, years passed without my noticing, and my grandmother became quite elderly and was approaching the end of her life.

Arrangements were made so she could spend most of her last months, weeks, and days in her own home surrounded by the things and the people she loved and that made her most comfortable.

I made quite a few trips during this period to the aforementioned Springfield. On what turned out to be my last visit, I arrived when she was already asleep for the night. Her nurse was sitting outside of her room and greeted me. I told her I wished I could have arrived earlier in the day, but a business commitment had delayed me. The nurse told me that my grandmother was aware of that and was very proud of the work I did.

This really surprised me as I had never known that my grandmother really understood what I did for a living. When you're the first entrepreneur in your family, it's a little hard for the elder generations to grasp the concept.

The nurse laughed softly, took my hand, and quietly led me through the doorway into my grandmother's room. The nurse whispered, "Beside her bed there is a picture of you holding the Emmy award you received. Every person who comes into this house receives the same explanation from your grandmother. She points to that picture and tells them, 'This is my grandson. He does two things—he helps blind people see television, and he travels around the world telling people they can have good things in their lives.'"

As impactful as that was at that time, the true import of it is still dawning upon me many years later. I didn't realize it at the time, and I'm quite certain my grandmother never heard of a personal mission statement, but without realizing it, through a private duty night nurse, my grandmother had given me my personal mission statement.

As I dictate these words, I am sitting in the office of my ever-growing business called the Narrative Television Network, and my most sincere desire is that these words are telling you that you can have good things in your life.

Anyone who has ever achieved a degree of what we would all call success has been on a mission. Their mission is clear, concise, and easily stated. John F. Kennedy gave us all a goal in the '60s—that we would put a man on the moon and bring him back to earth safely. That launched a mission for us all that culminated at the end of that same decade when Neil Armstrong stepped on the surface of the moon and returned to earth safely. Had you asked Neil Armstrong during that time about his mission, I'm quite certain it would have been stated very clearly that he was, indeed, on his way to the moon.

During the darkest days of World War II when Winston Churchill uttered some of the most profound statements ever voiced by a human being, he did more to win the war than anyone else. Churchill never fired a shot or captured an enemy soldier, but he won the war by defining our mission in terms that everyone understood. He articulated what our success would be and clarified that failure was intolerable.

Before you master productivity through motivation, communication, and implementation, it is vital that you define success and clarify your mission.

## CHAPTER FOUR

# THE ART OF A PRODUCTIVE LIFE

Productivity is probably one of the most misunderstood elements of success. *Productive* is a derivative of the word *produce*. It quite simply means to generate results. As we have already learned, in order to be successful you have to make choices, define success in your own terms, and create a mission that will take you toward your ultimate destiny; therefore, as we look at the Art of Productivity, it can only be gauged or measured in light of your personalized success goals.

Just because you're moving, it does not mean you're moving in the right direction. Visualize the hamster in the cage frantically running on the spinning wheel. He has a lot of activity but no productivity. If the hamster runs even faster, he still doesn't get anywhere.

Be careful to never confuse activity with productivity. Most people in our society work very hard in terms of activity, and we all fill 24 hours each day and seven days each week; but, as in the case of our hamster friend, just because we're running or even sprinting doesn't mean we're really moving at all in terms of productive progress toward our personalized success goal.

It is actually astonishing to realize that, in some cases, activity can be counterproductive. If you're moving down the highway at 70 miles per hour on a clear, bright, sunny day with very little traffic, you might think you're making good progress or being very productive. In reality, if your destination lies somewhere behind you in the opposite direction, your activity is actually counterproductive. In this case, going faster or working harder will take you even farther away from your goal or destination than you currently are. Someone pulled off to the side of the road who is not moving at all is actually making more progress, or being more productive, than you are.

The Art of Productivity is only applicable as it relates to your personalized success and your individual mission toward that destiny. Sometimes in the midst of frantic activity, the most productive thing you can do is stop, take a deep breath, and ask yourself several questions.

1. What is it I'm really trying to accomplish?

2. Do I really want to accomplish this?

3. Will this activity move me toward that end result?

4. Is there a better way to get from here to there than I am currently pursuing?

In a ready, aim, fire world, too often we overlook the *ready* and the *aim* portion of the equation. There's only one good reason to pursue any activity, and that is because it is the most productive and efficient way to accomplish your mission of moving toward your personal success goal.

Not long ago, I had an opportunity to train a team of sales people. These individuals were engaged in commission selling from cold calls and referrals. They had no responsibilities other than to sell their product. When I arrived on the scene, I first spent most of my time listening and observing their activity.

Too often, outside advisors and consultants come into a situation and perform ready, fire, aim consulting. Before you seek anyone's opinion, make sure they understand your unique success goal and the mission you have undertaken to get from here to there. Otherwise, you will get some great advice that may rapidly take you even farther away from where you want to be than you currently are.

As I observed these individual sales people, they all appeared to be working very hard. For the most part, they arrived at the office early, they seemed to be engaged in frantic activity, and—by and large—they stayed late into the work day. After gathering the information I needed, I called them all together and asked several questions.

1. How many hours a week do you work?

2. Are you working hard?

Their answers were quite revealing. The average sales person felt they were working about 45 to 50 hours a week, and they all assured me they were working extremely hard. Then I asked a simple question: What is your job here?

They responded in unison by letting me know their job was to sell their company's product. When I asked how they could accomplish this other than by talking to prospects on the phone or in person, it got very quiet.

So then I gave them the good news. I let them know that they could all make more money by generating more sales by only working 15 hours a week. This was greeted with great skepticism.

I got them each a discount store stopwatch and told them to keep it in their jacket pocket or purse during the workday. Anytime they were actually engaged talking to a prospect about their company's products or services, they were to click the watch on; and when they were done, they were to click the watch off until they began talking to another potential customer. I told them that once they had reached 15 hours of productive work time in the week, as indicated by their stopwatch, they were done until next week.

As I had already approved this with their supervisor, they were elated to find out they only had to work 15 hours per week. What they didn't realize was that the average sales person in that organization had actually only been working around five hours a week, and they had been wasting approximately 40 hours a week in non-productive activity.

A few months after they implemented this stopwatch productivity system, I got some feedback results. Approximately a third of the sales people were breaking their own previous records and many of the company's sales records. Approximately a third of the sales people were still working 45 hours a week in their old manner, which you and I now understand meant they were really only working productively five hours a week. And, finally, a third of the sales people had quit as they could not handle the unstructured freedom and responsibility of the Art of Productivity.

The top third of the sales force was only coming into the office a few hours each day. They were efficiently and productively establishing new customers, and then they were spending time with their families, fishing, or improving their golf game. Because their sales numbers were astounding to management, no one cared how many or how few hours they spent in the office.

Your professional work day is about creating productivity, not generating activity designed to convince someone that you're working. I realize that it is hard to define every job in every field in absolute terms of activity vs. productivity, but you know better than anyone else when you're making a difference and when you're just treading water for appearance's sake.

One of my heroes and mentors was the legendary Coach John Wooden. He passed away a few months before his one-hundredth birthday, and I was privileged to know him and work with him during the last decade of his life. You have heard it said that some wise people have forgotten more than anyone else knows. This would be true of Coach Wooden except for the fact that he never forgot anything, even as he approached a century of life.

In the totally-measurable, definable world of bigtime college basketball, Coach Wooden has more championships and created more success than anyone, ever. He dominated the college basketball landscape in a way that has never been equaled before or since.

He recruited and cultivated players such as Kareem Abdul-Jabbar, Bill Walton, and countless college and future NBA stars. Coach Wooden had a phrase that he shared with his players that I believe defines the Art of Productivity for us all. When Coach Wooden had a player who was not getting into position fast enough, he would repeat the phrase, "Be quick, but don't hurry."

As simple as this may seem, it can define the difference between your success and your failure. In Coach Wooden's terms, being quick means moving efficiently and under control toward your destination. Hurrying means being out of control and running with reckless abandon.

Being quick will get you into position to win. Hurrying will simply tire you out on the road to inevitable failure. Quickness is a state of mind. Hurrying is a state of activity.

Remember to never confuse activity with productivity. As you look at your daily, weekly, and monthly calendar, when you review each item ask yourself the question: Is this activity or productivity? This can only be judged in light of your firmly-established success goal and the mission you are on to take you there.

If you will learn to work smarter, not harder; quicker and not more hurried; and productively, not simply more actively, you will begin to live a life of productivity full of peace, serenity, joy, and success beyond your wildest dreams.

## CHAPTER FIVE

# THE ART OF CUSTOMIZING

I am an optimist. I believe that the biggest dream you ever had in your life is alive and well, and the only thing you have to do to activate it and eventually live it is to create the Art of Productivity through motivation, communication, and implementation. You have everything you need to live out your dreams. Your goal would not have been put inside of you unless you have the capacity to achieve it.

Having said that, just as your goal is totally unique to you in the way that you define success, and just as your mission to pursue that goal is yours alone, the tools, skills, and talents you bring to the task are totally unique.

One of the challenges with most success books, courses, or philosophies is the fact that some well-meaning person who may be successful is telling you how they have succeeded. My goal in *The Art of Productivity* book and the Ultimate Productivity Profile I have set up to help corporations and individuals find their unique path is to equip you to assess your own unique skill set in order to fulfill your own mission on the way to your defined success.

I created the Ultimate Productivity Profile in collaboration with my talented colleague Rebeka Graham who is one of the great corporate trainers in the world. Together, we drew upon knowledge, experience, and wisdom from top-level performers such as Steve Forbes, Coach John Wooden, and many others. As you read through this book, you and your colleagues will have the opportunity to take the Ultimate Productivity Profile and receive your individualized assessment.

As a blind person for over two decades, I have had to come to grips with the fact that I cannot do things the way I used to do them. If you were to poll a number of blind people as to their greatest limitations resulting from their disability, I believe many of them would mention two things. Reading and driving are perceived to be visual skills, and blind people suffer from their inability to engage in these activities.

In reality, when you understand the Art of Productivity, reading is not about visually seeing words on a page, and driving is not about operating a vehicle. Reading is the pursuit of information, and driving is simply a matter of getting from Point A to Point B.

As I explained to you previously, when I could read words on a page just as you are reading these words now, I don't believe I ever completed reading an entire book cover to cover; but now, thanks to a high speed digital player and recordings from the National Library for the Blind, I literally read a book every day.

I have never met a person who has read more books than I have. There probably are people who have, indeed, completed more books than me. I simply have never met them. I know that I would enjoy meeting such people, because the act of reading a book a day for over two decades has so expanded my world that I would love to meet people whose world has been expanded to a greater extent than mine.

With respect to driving, I have not operated a vehicle since the day—as a 16-year-old, newly licensed driver—I rear-ended a parked police car I didn't see. This is a bittersweet tale that I will save for another venue, but suffice it to say, that experience ended my active operation of a vehicle over 30 years ago; however, thanks to chauffeur-driven limousines as well as first-class and private air travel, I have gone anywhere around the world I have wanted to go and look forward to traveling even more in the future.

One must always remember that there is more than one way to skin a cat as my grandmother always told me.

Keep your goal in mind and realize that your mission is merely a way to get to your goal. Your goal should never waver or be altered, but your mission to reach that goal and the methods you employ should be totally flexible and constantly scrutinized in the light of the Art of Productivity.

I am told that each year there are several million quarter-inch drill bits sold in hardware stores and tool outlets around the world. I can safely say that no one ever really wanted a quarter-inch drill bit, even though millions of people buy them. They don't want the drill bit. What they want is a quarter-inch hole. If there were another method developed to magically create quarter-inch holes in any substance, I submit to you that the million-drill-bit-a-year market would dry up overnight.

Please remember that we always find what we are looking for. If you seek to have a great day, find a new opportunity, or meet the person who will make the difference in your personal or professional life, you will find them. On the other hand, if you get up tomorrow morning looking for a dull boring day, the same old regimen, and people who drain you of your energy instead of building you up toward your personal goal, this is, indeed, what you will find.

I hate to be the one to tell you this, but if you haven't figured it out already, it's time you knew that life is not fair. Life is great, it's grand, and it's wonderful, but it is not fair. In this life, we don't always get what we want. We don't always get what we need. We don't always get what we deserve. And we don't even always get what we earn. But we will, inevitably and unerringly, get exactly what we expect.

If your life today does not look like you want it to in every facet of your existence, simply examine your expectations, and you will find that somewhere along the way you came to expect the life that you are experiencing at this moment. That may be somewhat startling and disturbing to you, but take heart. If those expectations have brought you here, the expectations you will build and nurture through the Art of Productivity will take you anywhere you want to go.

Recently, I read a book by a well-meaning Ph.D. purporting to tell readers how to be a millionaire. Always remember, whether it's me or anyone else whose thoughts you read or listen to, don't ever take advice from anyone who doesn't have what you want. This particular Ph.D., on close examination, was not only not a millionaire, but—thanks to indiscriminate use of credit cards—he had a negative net worth. This, however, did not stop him from telling unsuspecting readers the single and true path to becoming a millionaire.

Among the 30-plus books I have written to date is my book *The Millionaire Map,* which tells my own story of moving from poverty to becoming a multimillionaire. You can find out more about this title and take a free Millionaire Assessment at www.TheMillionaireMap.com. When writing that book, I had to do one of the most difficult things I have ever done as a public person. I had to reveal my own net worth as audited by Bank of America and Merrill Lynch. You can review this financial verification at the website mentioned above. I was willing to overcome the discomfort of revealing my own decamillionaire status because I feel you, as a reader, have the right to know the track record of people who are showing you the way to success, wealth, or productivity.

Recent statistics tell us that there are over 9 million millionaires in the United States, and I can assure you that there are 9 million ways to reach that goal. They are all valid, but they are not interchangeable or transferable.

Michael Jordan found his way to becoming a multimillionaire through being arguably the greatest basketball player ever. In the prime of his career, he decided to pursue becoming a baseball player. His best efforts resulted in Michael Jordan becoming a mediocre Minor League baseball player. While it is remarkable that he could achieve even that status in baseball, it is exceedingly obvious that Michael Jordan's path to success was through basketball and, had he only ever played baseball and never explored other avenues and paths to success, you and I would have never heard the name Michael Jordan.

There is a unique path for you and me that will take us down a road where we find power, pleasure, and passion in the ongoing pursuit of our personal success. No matter how hard Michael Jordan might have worked in playing baseball, he would have never reached his personal success or mastered the Art of Productivity without getting off the baseball road and back onto the basketball road that led him to fame, fortune, and success.

Before you change your tires, tune up your car, and try to get in the fast lane, be sure you're on the right road going the right direction that will take you to your personal success.

## CHAPTER SIX

# THE ART OF PASSION

Before you and I make the quantum leap into motivation, communication, and implementation, which are the engines of the Art of Productivity, we have to take a brief detour to confirm you are on track with your personalized definition of success and your customized mission. Unless these elements fit you perfectly, you cannot reach your destination.

The only thing that will make you succeed is to create more value by utilizing the Art of Productivity. If you are going to go through the fire of achievement, you've got to make sure you're on the exclusive road that will take you to your personal destination. The only way to gauge your accuracy in this area is to examine your passion.

I have had the privilege of meeting and working with some of the greatest people of the 20th and now the 21st century either onstage, on television, in movies, or in interviews for my columns and books. Each of these people has reached the pinnacle in their arena of business, sports, politics, social change, or the world of entertainment.

These ultimate achievers come in many shapes and sizes, and there is only one element that I have been able to discern that they all have in common without fail. Each of these superstars has an unwavering and burning passion toward the personal goals they pursue.

My very first interview broadcast on the Narrative Television Network was with the legendary movie star Katharine Hepburn. We had several conversations after the interview, and I was in communication with her up until several months prior to her passing. Katharine Hepburn was a pioneer in the movie industry and received acclaim that was unparalleled both from her audiences and her peers.

I will never forget the feeling as a novice interviewer of sitting down that first time to talk with Katharine Hepburn. She was intimidating to me, to say the least, but totally down to earth and unassuming. Her answer to one of my questions remains indelibly etched in my mind.

I asked, "Miss Hepburn, if you had not found your way into show business as a movie actress, what field do you feel you would have pursued throughout your life?"

She considered my question for a moment and then responded hesitantly, "I'm not exactly sure what I would have done, but I hope I would have gone into medicine or some healing profession."

Then, with that unwavering degree of certainty that movie fans came to love, she continued emphatically, "If I had not been able to make a living as an actress, I would have had to have found another way to sustain myself as I acted to support my habit, because I act out of an innate need to be an actress."

This kind of passion will sustain you just as it did Katharine Hepburn through the trials and triumphs of pursuing your mission to reach your personal success. Everyone works hard and faces challenges and difficulties. Those people who prevail are those who are pursuing their own passion.

I am reminded of a story that I often have the opportunity to share from the arena stage at events around the world.

Once upon a time, there were two ancient tribes of people who lived in close proximity to one another. One tribe lived in a lush valley near a swiftly flowing river that sustained this valley tribe and their crops and livestock year 'round. The valley people lived an agrarian lifestyle of planting, cultivating, and harvesting throughout the seasons, year after year.

The second ancient tribe lived in the high-up mountains, just below the snowline where they dwelt in caves and sustained themselves through hunting for meat and furs. The mountain tribe prospered as they taught ensuing generations of their young people the art of hunting and trapping.

The two ancient tribes lived in different worlds. They rarely even sighted one another, even though they lived less than a day's travel on foot from each other. As often happens when two societies or groups of people don't communicate, the two tribes began to fear one another and be suspicious of the other tribe. When human beings fail to communicate and understand one another, they always assume the worst to be true.

Then, one day, some misguided youth from the mountain tribe strayed beyond their normal hunting grounds. As teenagers will often do, without thinking they acted. These teenagers took a young baby that was sleeping on a pallet near the river where its mother and the other ladies of the valley tribe were washing clothes.

Before they realized it, the teenagers from the mountain tribe were running along the path through the woods that led back to their mountain home, carrying the baby. When they saw they were being pursued from a distance by the women of the valley tribe, before they knew it the teenage hunters from the mountain tribe had gone beyond the point of no return, and they went back to their cave dwellings with the baby they had kidnapped.

They hadn't unintentionally kidnapped just any baby. This was the infant son of the chief of the valley tribe.

That very night, there was an emergency council meeting of the valley tribe around the bonfire. The chief implored his greatest warriors to climb up the mountain and bring back his baby. At daybreak, the best and strongest warriors from the valley tribe headed up the mountain in pursuit of their chief's son. They were brave and determined but were not accustomed to the mountain terrain and, by sundown, they returned dejectedly to the valley campsite and their forlorn chief.

With the last rays of the setting sun, the chief and the people of the valley tribe spotted a lone figure coming down the mountain that their warriors had been unable to climb. As the figure approached, it was revealed to be the chief's wife, holding her baby son in her arms.

There was great rejoicing throughout the tribe, and when the celebration subsided, the chief asked his wife in the hearing of all those assembled, "How is it that you, my wife, could climb that mountain and return with our child when our best and bravest warriors failed?"

She smiled and replied with the answer that rings true for you and me, "It wasn't their baby."

Your personal success goal had better be fully in line with your deepest passion. The fact that your mother wants you to go to college, your spouse wants you to lose weight, and your boss wants you to produce more doesn't matter when we are considering the Art of Productivity as it relates to your mission and your personal success through motivation, communication, and implementation.

Motivation, communication, and implementation represent powerful tools, but they will only work for you if it's your baby. You will know, deep down, whether it's your baby if you have the passion and the fire inside of you to get up that mountain of your personal success.

Few people ever find and pursue their true passion, so it's easier to see daily examples around us of people mired down in mediocrity far removed from their personal success and passion.

I once worked with a gentleman who could barely drag himself to work 30 to 45 minutes late each day and, somehow, slog through his day's tasks in slow motion. He was tired, depressed, and dejected each day, and many around him questioned whether he would get out of bed and do it again the next morning. But then one day, he asked me to go fishing, and

I discovered an amazing lesson about passion, courtesy of this gentleman.

The same guy who arrived each morning in a zombie state around 10:00 a.m. told me he would be picking me up for our fishing trip on Saturday at 3:00 a.m. I'm an early riser. I'm listening to my high-speed audiobooks most mornings by 4:15 or 4:30, but 3:00 a.m. is an hour I rarely experience; however, the prospect of observing my under-energetic friend at that forsaken hour intrigued me, so on Saturday morning at 3:00 a.m. sharp when his truck pulled into my driveway, I got into the cab of his truck expecting the worst.

I received the surprise of my life when I was greeted by one of the most enthusiastic, energetic, passionate people I had ever met. By 4:30, we were wading thigh-deep in a freezing stream, and he was a nonstop bundle of joy all day. With a few brief breaks for food and water, he was a constant fishing machine, on fire until long after the sun set. As we drove home, he gave me an excited blow-by-blow recap of his entire 13 hours of fishing that day.

As we approached my house and he dropped me off, it dawned on me that we had found his passion or his power groove.

When I was in high school, I thought I wanted to be a professional football player, but when I was diagnosed with the condition that eventually robbed me of my eyesight, I knew I would never make the NFL; so

I became a competitive Olympic weightlifter and actually won a national championship for my weight class and age division.

Among weightlifters, it is well known that there is a power groove, which is a very narrow range of motion in which weightlifters are significantly stronger than the average person; however, if the strongest weightlifter in the world gets a few inches out of his power groove, his strength diminishes geometrically.

Your and my professional and personal lives are the same way. If we live, move, and have our being within the realm of our passion, we are unbeatable; but if we get out of our power groove, like the passionate fisherman on an average workday in the office, we are doomed to failure.

George Burns told me that if you love your job, you never have to work a day in your life.

I got to interview the golf legend Lee Trevino late in his career. He told me after many consecutive weeks of playing competitive golf he would come home, throw his golf clubs in the garage, and tell anyone who would listen, "I'm never going to play golf again." But after a good night's sleep, he was generally rummaging around in the garage, loading up his golf clubs, and heading out to get on a golf course somewhere. He shrugged and sheepishly explained, "Jim, I just love to play golf."

Probably the highlight of my celebrity interviews was the afternoon I spent with Frank Sinatra. No one before or since has dominated show business for half a century like Frank Sinatra did. There was an amazing energy around Mr. Sinatra.

He and his entourage had taken over the top several floors of a major hotel complex in preparation for a concert he was doing that night. The street had been barricaded for several blocks around the hotel, and security was extremely tight. News helicopters were flying around the hotel, and it was an amazing environment.

I remember commenting to Mr. Sinatra and several of his people that they had created quite a stir in Dallas. Mr. Sinatra was a bit perplexed and bewildered and asked one of his confidants, "Do you know what this guy's talking about?"

The nearest bodyguard/assistant replied, "Yes, sir. I do, but you probably don't."

Then it dawned on me. For his entire adult life, Frank Sinatra had never been anywhere that wasn't receiving the same Frank Sinatra effect that Dallas was experiencing that day. He thought the chaos was normal. We had a great interview, and he epitomized passion in several ways.

I asked him, as a movie star, recording artist, TV personality, and so much more, how he would like to be remembered. He said he would like to be remembered as a guy telling a simple story through a song that made people feel things.

As I was getting ready to leave after the interview, he called out to me with words I'll never forget. "Hey, kid. I hope you live to be a hundred years old, and the last thing you ever hear is me singing you a song."

May you and I similarly find our own passions in life.

## CHAPTER SEVEN

# THE ART OF DISCOVERY

In the entire continuum from first becoming aware that you have choices and can act on them to completing your mission and living your dreams through your personal success, there are many rungs on the ladder.

I want to congratulate you for defining success on your own terms, establishing a mission from where you are to where you want to be, and examining your destination in light of your passion. You're well on your way to living out your dreams, but it's important to realize that many people have had dreams, set goals, and launched into a mission. The greatest disconnect along the road to success are the practical steps that involve motivation, communication, and implementation.

You may have a lifelong dream or a ten-year goal, and these things are valid, but it all comes down to taking that first step. You've heard it said that a journey of a thousand miles begins with a single step. I'll go one further and submit to you that a journey of a thousand miles is nothing more than a series of single steps. If you stop or take a detour on any one of those steps, you will not reach your destination.

Through my speeches, syndicated column, and books, I have the privilege of meeting and corresponding with countless people who have lofty goals and worthwhile dreams. They have a plan that takes them far into the future, but unfortunately they don't have a plan that takes into account this day, this hour, or this moment.

Those of you who are familiar with my work or have read another of my 30 or so books are most likely familiar with *The Ultimate Gift* or the 20th Century Fox movie based on that novel I wrote. For some reason, that story of an elderly man's desire to pass on his knowledge and wisdom and not just his riches has resonated with many millions of people around the world.

In the movie, the elderly gentleman—Red Stevens who knows he is nearing the end of his life—is played by the legendary actor James Garner. Garner, through the character Red Stevens, leaves behind 12 videotaped messages for his grandson, dealing with the 12 pivotal life lessons as he sees them.

In the aftermath of the successful movie and millions of *Ultimate Gift* books in print, people ask me which of the 12 gifts is most important in life. When you consider the gift of money, work, friends, family, love, and several others, it's hard to pick just one. But if I were forced to pick the most important gift as it relates to you achieving your personal success, it would invariably be the Gift of a Day.

In the Gift of a Day, you begin to recognize that, at best, life is very short. Even if you live to what we consider to be an old age, it flies by in the blink of an eye. Having a successful life is nothing more than stringing together a series of successful years. A successful year is simply a matter of laying down 12 successful months. A successful month takes nothing more than the establishment of four successful weeks, and a successful week is made up of a series of successful days. But, when it's all said and done, the only day that matters is today. Yesterday is a canceled check, and tomorrow is little more than a promissory note. Today is cash. It is real, it is tangible, and you and I have to spend it wisely.

For almost 20 years, I have written a weekly column that is read by people through newspapers, magazines, and online publications around the world. My column is entitled *Winners' Wisdom*, and each week I try to deliver just that—a piece of wisdom that, if applied, will create winners. Every one of these columns ends with a single phrase: "Today's the Day!"

When my publisher put together a compilation of these columns in book form, they gave it the title *Wisdom for Winners*. Subsequently, they have also released *Wisdom for Winners Volume Two* simply because you can read about, hear about, or learn of wisdom, but unless you apply it, it doesn't matter. It's simply knowledge with no energy. Once you apply that knowledge, it becomes wisdom, and the only time you can apply wisdom in your life is today.

I'm not as interested in the specifics of your personal goal or your mission to get there as I am in your activity today. Every day is a gift, and you get one day closer to or one day further from your goal. If you work like, act like, and have an attitude like someone who is on the way to achieving your personal goal, you are already successful.

The great hotel baron, Conrad Hilton, was once asked when he knew he would be successful. He told the reporter he knew he would be successful when he was still penniless and sleeping on a park bench, because he was doing the things it took to reach his personal success.

Today is all you have to invest in your future. If you're going to succeed, you're going to do so by employing the success elements of motivation, communication, and implementation. Everyone who has ever succeeded has done so with these principles whether or not they defined them in the terms that you and I are defining them.

Motivation is the fuel that makes your mission toward your personal success possible. Motivation is the first thing we get when we come into this life and the last thing that slips away as we leave. We do everything we do—good or bad—because, for one reason or another, we are motivated to do so. Recognizing that today is the only thing you have to invest toward your success, if you haven't been investing wisely, you have to change your motivation.

Communication is the way you define and share your mission and personal success for yourself and those around you. No one has ever succeeded by themselves. If someone tells you they have never failed at anything, you can confidently let them know that, if nothing else, at a minimum they have failed to recognize the contribution of others.

Unless you can communicate your goals, you really don't own them, and you haven't firmly established them in your own mind. Great educators will tell you that the best way to learn a subject is to teach it. The very process of communicating a lesson drives it deeper into your mind and into your soul.

You will need to build a success team. They cannot draw on your passion. They can only draw on what you communicate. What you feel, think, or believe is meaningless unless you can share it. This can only be done through communication.

Implementation is putting your thoughts, dreams, passions, mission, and personal success goals into action. When it's all said and done in our world, there's a lot more said than done. You will not live out your dreams because you meant to act today or because you intended to take the right steps. Your best intentions are meaningless. You will reap the rewards of the Art of Productivity.

If you meant to cook dinner but didn't, you will be hungry. If you meant to light the fire but you failed to act, you will be cold. And, just as certainly, if you don't implement your mission on a daily basis, you will fail.

I wish I could give you the blueprint for your own motivation, communication, and implementation; however, these elements are as individual to you as your fingerprints. Fortunately, you hold the keys to these blueprints of your own motivation, communication, and implementation as well as those members of your success team you will be drawing toward you.

You may think you're motivating an associate by drawing attention to their accomplishments in front of a vast audience. In reality, that may be terrifying, demoralizing, and de-motivating to that individual. In this case, your best intentions will be taking you farther away from your intended goal. You may think you're communicating your mission to those around you who have accepted the task of creating the Art of Productivity and success; however, if you're communicating in English and they all speak French, or if you're communicating in writing and they can't read, you're not going to succeed.

Remember, as a blind person I can't see the words, but I read more than anyone I know via audio books. If you were trying to communicate with me but insisted on doing it through black on white, ink on paper, you and I could not succeed.

Finally, if you are trying to implement yourself or engage those around you in beginning a task, you've got to understand how everyone, collectively, achieves their maximum performance in order to create the Art of Productivity.

If you and your team were committed to the task of rebuilding and restoring the Statue of Liberty as was done several years ago, you would have to motivate your team to give their best efforts to preserve this symbol of our freedom and all it means. You would have to communicate your passion for the project and your instructions for everyone involved, but unless you could implement, nothing that had gone before would really matter.

If you and your team decided that you were going to begin working at 6:00 a.m., but then you discovered that the first ferry boat did not run out to the island where the Statue of Liberty is located until 9:00 a.m., you simply couldn't implement.

More people fail due to misguided motivation, chaotic communication, and inappropriate implementation than anything else.

# CHAPTER EIGHT

# THE ART OF ASSESSMENT

As an athlete, businessperson, and success speaker, I have had the privilege of studying winners and losers for several decades. The difference between winners and losers is relatively minor on the productivity side and overwhelming on the reward side.

As I have studied success and those who make it happen in the corporate arena, investment field, and the world of entrepreneurship, it resurfaces time after time that the winning edge invariably happens when the elements of motivation, communication, and implementation all come together. For this reason, I have put together this book and an Ultimate Productivity Profile that entrepreneurs, investors, and those in the corporate world utilize to bring motivation, communication, and implementation into focus.

Although you have established your own definition of success that drives you—your specific mission to get you from here to there as well as the passion that will carry you through over the long haul—without the practical elements of motivation, communication, and implementation you will be all dressed up with nowhere to go. These elements are vital to everyone but are individual in the way they must be brought to bear upon your specific situation.

Let's say you are getting into your dress-for-success mode and want a custom suit made for you so you can look and feel your best. No matter how motivated your tailor may be; no matter how much you communicate to him or her the style, fabric, and design you want; and no matter how willing and able your tailor is to begin implementing the process, without knowing and understanding your specific measurements, you don't have a chance of ever getting a top-of-the-line, tailor-made suit.

Many leaders around the world have been intricately involved with the development of the Ultimate Productivity Profile, which allows individuals and those they work with to understand their own specific strengths as they relate to motivation, communication, and implementation.

One of my great influences in developing the Ultimate Productivity Profile has been legendary Coach John Wooden. No one has ever been more successful at putting together a winning team than Coach Wooden. He did it year after year with different circumstances and different players. Coach Wooden helped me understand that motivation, communication, and implementation are imperative, but you must work with each player and every team differently.

Some players are motivated by a pat on the back. Other players need their pat a little lower and a bit harder. Some players need verbal communication, and others have to see a diagram of the play drawn out on a board. Some players implement best with long, rigorous practices while others need several sessions a day.

There are many ways, styles, and vehicles that can get you to your destination. If you are committed to a certain vehicle or a certain route instead of being committed to success, itself, your odds of living out your dreams or experiencing your destiny are very low.

I get on an airplane numerous times each month. I was extremely concerned to learn when talking to a pilot once that, during a two-hour flight, he is off course the vast majority of the time. When a flight plan is filed and he logs all of the trip information into the computer, the computer onboard virtually maps out the perfect flight from where the plane is currently to its intended destination. Unfortunately, from the point of takeoff until the point of landing, that plane is either too high, too low, or off course to the left or right constantly. If you fly regularly, you'll be thankful to know, as I was, that the onboard computer and the pilot constantly correct the course.

If they were only committed to the computerized model instead of being committed to their destination, the minute they got off course they would simply circle around, land at the airport where they just took off, and try again later.

No one who succeeded ever got there exactly the way they thought they would. Even if things go exactly according to your plan, conditions between here and there are changing constantly.

Coach Wooden realized that there are certain absolutes in the game of basketball. You've got to score more points than the other team during the time allotted for the game. Beyond that, there are as many ways to motivate, communicate, and implement as there are players who have ever played the game.

Coach Wooden had a specific pattern for the way he coached his teams and the roles each player was to fulfill. Then, he recruited a player named Lou Alcindor. Lou Alcindor was taller, quicker, and possessed unique skills that were different from virtually anyone who had ever played the game. The goal of winning by scoring more points than the other team in the prescribed time for the game never changed; however, Coach Wooden realized that, within his system, he needed to be flexible to utilize the tremendous talent and potential of this new player.

Lou Alcindor went on to be among the greatest college basketball players of all time, and Coach Wooden led those teams to National Championships because he adapted the way he motivated, communicated, and implemented with Lou Alcindor and the other members of that team in a way that brought out their Art of Productivity. Lou Alcindor rewrote the record books in the NBA and became known as Kareem Abdul-Jabbar.

The people in your office or on your team have as much talent and potential as Kareem Abdul-Jabbar did as a basketball player, but you're going to have to understand who they are and the way you can produce the Art of Productivity through unique motivation, communication, and implementation that suits them. Success is never a one-size-fits-all proposition. It is a custom-tailored, one-of-a-kind, magnificent suit lovinlgy made with no one in mind other than you.

As a blind person myself and as the president of the Narrative Television Network, which makes movies, television, and educational programming accessible for our nation's 13 million blind and visually impaired people, I have long been involved in the field of special education. For many years, the field of special education did not exist. Students who had disabilities that did not allow them to function in the expected, standard way within the classroom simply did not receive an education. Then, as specific disabilities became more understood within the medical and educational communities, the field of special education was born.

Students who could not function in the standard— or what was thought of as normal—way became known as having a learning disability. The term *learning disabled* permeated the field for many years, and I feel limited opportunities for untold numbers of students who were not given the customized tools and specific encouragement needed to reach their potential.

More recently, a new term has emerged within the field of special education. Today, these students are known to have a learning difference, not a disability. The labeling alone has made a huge difference because we all have a tendency to live up to labels and the expectations that are attached to them. The term *learning disabled* denotes a student with a disability or a problem that does not allow them to function up to par. The term *learning difference* denotes a unique person who may need to take an alternative route to get to the same destination or possibly even a greater destination than their peers. Learning disability defines a deficiency in the student. Learning difference alerts the teacher to seek new ways to motivate, communicate, and implement with this individual.

This is true when we think about ourselves and those we work with. If you try to work exactly like everyone around you or try to get everyone around you to work exactly like you, you will never reach your own definition of success through the Art of Productivity.

Hammers, screwdrivers, and wrenches are all irreplaceable tools for a carpenter, but they are hardly interchangeable. The best carpenter in the world will have his productivity diminished or halted completely if he tries to drive nails with a screwdriver. If Coach Wooden thought that Kareem Abdul-Jabbar should play point guard and dribble the ball down the court while the five-foot-ten point guard played center, I don't believe the championship banners that are displayed at UCLA would be there.

At my company, Narrative Television Network, I believe we have the best team in the world. I hope you feel that way about your team. NTN has logistical people, accounting people, technical TV production people, and creative people. They are all vital, and I believe they are the very best at what they do, but they are hardly interchangeable.

It seems to be a universal law that the more someone excels in one area, the less competence they have in others. The Art of Productivity in any specific field requires talent, hard work, and dedication. By necessity, the further you climb up the ladder in one area, the less altitude you're able to achieve in others.

I was a weightlifter, which is a competitive sport in the Olympics. In the summer Olympics, there are also sprinters, gymnasts, and swimmers. These are elite, high-performance, ultimate productivity athletes within their own fields; but if you have a weightlifter competing in a swimming event, or a gymnast entered in the weightlifting competition, you are more likely to experience comedy than competitive drama.

As I dictate these words, they are being typed into a computer by an extremely talented grammarian, Dorothy Thompson, without whom no one would have read even one of my books or weekly syndicated columns. I am quite certain of this because I don't know how to type and, as an avid consumer of audio books, I have no knowledge or understanding of spelling or punctuation. This has not, however, kept me—with Dorothy's help—from selling millions and millions of books.

Downstairs in our building, we have four state-of-the-art digital TV editing studios. I don't know how to even turn that equipment on, but I run a successful television network. I have received an Emmy Award from the National Academy of Television Arts and Sciences recognizing NTN's engineering expertise, and I don't even know the names of the various pieces of equipment in our own facilities. Please don't tell the Academy!

If you are going to become the master of your own success goal by utilizing the Art of Productivity through motivation, communication, and implementation, you're going to have to pursue your passion by doing the things where you excel. You're going to need to recognize these same elements in everyone around you so that each player on your team is a world-class champion in their own area.

You become unstoppable and your personalized success goal becomes a certainty when you establish your own unique profile and that of those around you within the Art of Productivity. If you and every member of your team is functioning within your passion, utilizing your power groove with total communication and maximum implementation, your life becomes a fully fueled rocket ship that will launch you into a universe far beyond your wildest dreams.

It all begins with motivation.

CHAPTER NINE

# THE ART OF MOTIVATION

Whether you are pursuing your personal goal through the corporate world, entrepreneurship, or investing, you will have to understand motivation, communication, and implementation as it relates to you and everyone around you if you are to achieve the Art of Productivity.

Oftentimes, the hardest person to understand is ourself. Too many of us have a tendency to live in the past because we know all of our own shortcomings and keep repeating to ourselves all of our past stumbles and continually drag them into our future.

We are not the person we were in the past unless we choose to be. Even if you have experienced multiple failures before, you are no longer that person because you have the wisdom and the knowledge that have come from those experiences. You have heard it said that insanity is continually doing the same thing and expecting a different result. Conversely, wisdom dictates that if a certain behavior has brought us failure, we simply need to change the behavior in order to alter our future.

Once you have identified and connected with yourself and how to best utilize motivation, communication, and implementation in your individual world, you've got to be committed to continually monitoring the changes in your own life and how they impact you.

Shakespeare may have said it best when he wrote, "To thine own self be true." Like all great wisdom, this is exceedingly simple to say and unbelievably difficult to master. You'll be happy to know that you do not have to achieve perfection in order to enjoy your personal success. Some of my favorite baseball players have gone into the Hall of Fame by failing more times at the plate than they succeeded.

Donald Trump has always meant a lot to me and is an example, a role model, and a mentor. I have learned a great deal from him, both by watching his successes and his setbacks. When Donald succeeds, he does it on a grand scale, and when he stumbles, he does it the same way; but, like you and I must do, he gets up, brushes himself off, and begins again.

In the process of mastering motivation on your way to your personal success through the Art of Productivity, you've got to determine the most productive way to constantly motivate yourself as well as each individual person with whom you work. Remember, whether you spend your work day locked in a small office in your basement typing on a computer or in the middle of a mega-corporation surrounded by many thousands of colleagues, we all work with ourselves and work with others. We've got to pull the maximum motivational trigger for everyone, and it is not a one-size-fits-all proposition.

Let's start with the premise that you probably don't understand what motivates you, and you certainly don't get accurate feedback regarding what motivates your colleagues, coworkers, and associates. The higher up the ladder you are and the more important you are to those with whom you work, the more difficult it is to get accurate feedback.

If the CEO of a corporation asks everyone in the building how they like his tie on any given day, how often do you think he's going to get accurate and constructive feedback? If that same CEO spends considerable time, effort, energy, and money developing a strategy or program to motivate all of his people and then presents it in a company-wide meeting, he is likely to be showered with compliments and applause, regardless of what they really think.

I have worked with many top corporations and am constantly amazed to discover how little those who make the decisions know about how best to motivate the people for whom they are responsible. People are not exactly lying. They are giving answers and feedback that they feel is in their own enlightened self-interest.

If you're at your family Thanksgiving dinner and, in front of the whole tribe, Aunt Matilda asks you what you think of her baked squash casserole, I suspect—even if you think Aunt Matilda's baked squash casserole tastes like wallpaper paste—you're going to come up with some kind of an answer that is at least neutral if not positive.

Just as people want to preserve Aunt Matilda's feelings, they certainly want to preserve their job, livelihood, and family's financial security; therefore, it is important to realize that if you're the boss, you're probably not getting accurate feedback on how best to motivate your people.

This creates a false environment where nothing ever changes. If you're going to reach your personal success goal through the Art of Productivity utilizing motivation, communication, and implementation, you're going to have to be honest with yourself and those around you, and you're going to have to create an environment where people are comfortable being honest with you.

The term *motivation* is among the most misunderstood terms in our business and success vocabulary. For years, people have labeled me a motivational speaker, columnist, or author. While I understand the title and even appreciate their intentions, it is important to note that I don't motivate anyone, nor does anyone else. The most you can hope to do is find someone's hot button or something that resonates within an area inside their soul where they are already motivated.

Remember, we can never succeed by confusing activity with productivity. If all you want is frantic activity, you can get your people to appear motivated through fear, intimidation, or coercion. You could walk into your office tomorrow and tell everyone with a threatening tone that you are going to begin terminating people until the corporate motivation level improves. What you will get is a group of people who will smile, act busy, and probably say, "Yes, sir" or "Yes, ma'am," but you have not motivated anyone. In fact, you have actually de-motivated everyone.

Your intentions to motivate those around you will fail and even be counterproductive if they are not specific, targeted, mutually beneficial, and sincere. You may think you're motivating one of your associates by recognizing their birthday and telling them how much they mean to you and your organization. While this seems like a motivating gesture, if their birthday was seven-and-one-half months ago, you will have an individual who is less motivated than they were before.

### *Motivation has got to be specific.*

Many years ago, I am certain a football coach somewhere read that rousing music could motivate his team. So for many years, players suited up while listening to what their coach thought was motivating. The last time I visited a football locker room before a big game, it was as silent as a morgue. Some of the players were lounging, others were stretching, while still others were reviewing play books. Most of the players were wearing headsets attached to their iPods.

I later learned from the trainer that some of the players before a game liked to listen to loud rock music on their headsets while others listened to rap, classical, jazz, and every imaginable style of music. Still other players listened to sound effects of an ocean, a forest, or simply white noise. And still other players preferred silence.

If you simply assumed one thing was motivating for everyone, you would have failed miserably to motivate and would have actually de-motivated many of the players.

One of the things my late great friend and colleague Zig Ziglar said is that motivation is individualized, and it is in constant demand. He told me he had met a gentleman who explained to him he didn't need to go to a motivational meeting because he had been to many of them and had heard it all. Zig asked him if he took a shower today. The gentleman in question was a bit bewildered but nodded in the affirmative and let Zig know he had taken a shower. Zig told him that motivation was a bit like taking a shower. The shower you took last week, last month, or last year has probably worn off by now.

My university training is in the fields of psychology and sociology. Much of the current thinking would tell us that we human beings do everything we do for one of two reasons: To either gain pleasure or to avoid pain. While these are certainly valid motivators, I would submit that the majority of people you see daily commuting on the freeways, subways, or sidewalks are going back to their job—just as they did yesterday and the day before—more out of a sense of habit and routine than any form of motivation.

At one point in the past, they may have been motivated by their job, or at least they were more motivated about getting a job than starving to death; however, this is far from the motivation that you and I seek to reach our personal success through the Art of Productivity.

Remember, whether you work in the largest corporation in the world, a small business, or by yourself as an entrepreneur or investor, we all are part of a team, and only those of us who recognize this fact can succeed by achieving the Art of Productivity.

Your team is much like a jumbo jet airliner. There may be 400 people onboard, all going to the same destination; however, there are as many different motivations for the trip as there are people in the seats. The pilot, co-pilot, and flight attendants are doing their jobs; however, some members of the crew may have a total passion for flying or serving the traveling public while others are simply marking time—putting in their hours—because they don't know what else to do.

Among the passengers onboard, you might find people going to weddings, funerals, graduations, vacations, moving to or from a new city, or a myriad of other motivating factors. There will be people onboard for whom this flight will be an unforgettable experience because it is taking them to a once-in-a-lifetime event. They may be sitting next to a tired, bored businessperson who is on their fourth or fifth flight of the week.

I have met people who think they are motivated by money, but in reality they are motivated by their perception of what money can do for them in their lives. Money is a poor motivator unless it is attached to the vision of what the money will do for you. Some of the saddest people I know are trying to put more zeroes on their bank statement each month. Unless the pursuit of money is attached to college tuition, comfortable retirement, exciting travel, philanthropic gifts, financial security, or a myriad of other valid utilizations, this pursuit of money is the sign of a serious disease called MORE.

If all you want is more money, but you have not defined a significant use for that money, you are like the guy trying to put more gas in a tank that is already full, in a car that has no destination. A vehicle and fuel are useless if you don't have a personal goal. A nicer vehicle and more fuel will not solve your challenge. You've got to find that personal goal that sends you on a lifelong mission with passion. Then you will have achieved the Art of Productivity.

It is hard to imagine that money could even be a motivation for some people. I am proud to say that I consider Steve Forbes among my friends. He is a respected colleague and a valuable example and encourager to me. I cannot imagine Steve Forbes being motivated by money, other than as a means to keep score as he strives to improve himself and his organization.

Steve Forbes was born with more money than most of us will ever have or even imagine. One of the many reasons I admire him is the fact that he recognizes that his role in the world is to provide service and value to his colleagues and customers. He knows that the eventual result of providing this service and creating value in the lives of others is that he and those around him will make more money. But the money, in and of itself, is not a motivator—only what it can do or what it represents.

Most people, individually or corporately, make the mistake of looking at each task or objective as a series of questions. They look at: What are we doing, where are we doing it, who are we doing it with, how are we doing it, and when do we start? These are all critical questions that should be answered right after you answer the question that the motivation portion of the Art of Productivity demands, which is the overarching question: Why are we doing this? If the answer to that question doesn't motivate you and those around you, find something else to do.

## CHAPTER TEN

# THE ART OF MOTIVATIONAL MIRACLES

I began my business career as a broker for a New York Stock Exchange member firm. I had my own office in a relatively small town and was given the freedom to work independently as if I were an entrepreneur. In that field during the 1980s, there were tremendous promotions run by mutual funds, insurance companies, and large brokerage firms to get people like me to market their investment products and services.

Every few days, I was offered the opportunity to win a trip, a car, a cruise, and every imaginable inducement to capture my attention and that of brokers across the country. This was before the Internet revolutionized the investment and financial planning world. Virtually all of my critical information was printed out on a bulky, noisy, temperamental machine we called the night wire.

Each morning when I arrived at my office, there would be a printout laying on the floor that often would stretch 30 or 40 feet. The night wire told brokers across the country what new stocks and bonds were available, what special contests and promotions were offered, as well as performance numbers for individual brokers' sales. It was fascinating to observe which broker's sales numbers shot up at what time.

I found it comical that Bill or Fred would sell millions of dollars of oil and gas partnerships just to win what I thought was a dumb trip to Chicago. I would laugh to myself, thinking that with a fraction of the commissions they earned for those sales, they could travel around the world; but somehow a free trip to Chicago had motivated them. I certainly felt that I was not vulnerable to these kinds of tawdry commercial motivational tactics.

Then one morning, we were going over the night wire and it announced that any broker that sold several million dollars' worth of a new bond offering would receive six prime steaks overnighted to their office, packed in dry ice, and a bottle of French champagne.

By the end of the following day, I had broken all of my own sales records and most of the records for the entire firm before I realized that while I had been making fun of other brokers about their getting hooked by a gimmick, I had done the same thing, only worse. I didn't get a trip to Chicago or anywhere else. I simply got a box of frozen meat and a bottle of carbonated alcohol.

Then I began to realize that motivation is among the most individualized, personalized human traits. We spend inordinate amounts of time and money tracking what people do, and very little effort and energy determining why they do it.

If the CEO of my firm had called me and asked if I were excited about the possibility of winning a trip to Chicago, I would have immediately responded with a simple, "Yes, sir." Then I would have gone back to my office and done nothing out of the ordinary for the next few days as a result of that promotion. In fact, I probably would have been de-motivated, because I would have been thinking about how absurd it was that they thought I was going to go out of my way and make an extraordinary effort for a trip I had no interest in taking.

On the other hand, by the next week brokers across America were all reading their night wire, wondering why in the world I broke records to win a package of frozen steak and champagne that they wouldn't have gone across the street to get for free.

For this reason, I have—in conjunction with some of the greatest performance masters of our time—developed the Ultimate Productivity Profile. This brief survey tool allows people to assess their own motivational triggers and those of the people with whom they are associated. The Ultimate Productivity Profile is non-threatening in that there are no right or wrong answers. It simply identifies internal and external factors that cause us to perform.

The Ultimate Productivity Profile can give more accurate and detailed information in 20 minutes about how to motivate yourself and those around you than you can get in 20 years of a standard work environment relationship. Remember, honest people will rarely, if ever, lie to you, but seldom will they share their deepest, darkest true feelings with you, assuming they even understand them themselves.

I have a friend and colleague who for many years ran a billion-dollar corporation employing several thousand people. He became legendary by implementing a policy of taking an annual corporate trip. Once a year, every employee from the janitor to the CEO would be given an all-expenses-paid corporate trip for them and a guest. Employees who had been in the company for

10 years or 10 minutes were all treated the same. Everybody got the free trip.

It was front page news every year when four or five 747s flew into town and took all of my friend's employees and guests on an all-expenses-paid trip to Las Vegas, Disney World, or another exciting destination.

I remember an enlightening breakfast meeting I had with my friend when I inquired how he was able to afford such a corporate extravagance. He shared with me that the trips cost about $1,000 per year for each employee; therefore, he budgeted approximately $20 per week for each member of his entire corporate staff.

When I began to understand the scope of the motivation provided for the cost expended, I was astounded. Imagine if instead of my friend offering you an all-expenses-paid trip for you and a guest to a fantastic location, he told you that you were going to receive an additional $20 a week. If this caught your attention at all, it would probably be de-motivating in that it might seem like a paltry sum to present to you in recognition for all of your hard work.

On the other hand, my friend's employees were super motivated, tremendously loyal, and very proud to work for an organization that had an outstanding reputation in the community, because everybody knew that all of those employees got to go on the annual free trip.

It's important to realize that to create more motivation in your life or the lives of those around you,

you don't necessarily have to spend more money, more energy, or more time. You have to find their individual and collective motivational buttons and push them.

During the mid-1990s, I was invited to tour one of the hottest and fastest-growing among the dot-com companies of that time. They were experiencing meteoric success, and their biggest challenge was attracting and retaining qualified people to do all the work they were generating. This company had a tremendous amount of cash on hand, a profit picture that would be the envy of any enterprise, and unbelievable positive potential stretching out into the future.

As I arrived for my special tour, I was anticipating a palatial office with plush appointments and state-of-the-art technology. As my assistant and I were escorted into the main lobby, we were nearly struck by a young man in his 20s wearing Bermuda shorts and a tank top, riding a skateboard barefooted at an unbelievable rate of speed. I was shocked when I realized my host and tour guide didn't even seem to notice this unprecedented behavior within a corporate setting.

Then we were escorted into a huge area where the computer programmers worked. There were basketball goals, a volleyball net, and a trampoline in the middle of computer cubicles that were decorated more like a college dorm than a traditional setting in corporate America. There was loud music blaring, snack trays conveniently and liberally available throughout the work area, and I received a cordial invitation to participate in something they called the Friday beer bash.

I was already beginning to feel a bit like Alice in Wonderland taking a tour of a world with which I was not familiar, so without thinking I agreed to attend the aforementioned beer bash.

Apparently every Friday afternoon, this successful corporation would bring in kegs of beer, hire a local band, and have a function that more resembled a fraternity party than what I had previously thought of as a corporate function. As I was preparing to tell the CEO I didn't understand what was going on, it dawned on me that I didn't understand his people and what motivated them. I later learned that this particular corporation got more hours of productive work and bottom line profitability out of each employee than anyone in their industry.

While these tactics would have spelled an instant failure in the world of accounting or investment banking, it was an absolute prescription for success within the exploding world of technology at that time.

When I asked the CEO how in the world he had devised such a plan for his people, he chuckled and gave me the answer that became the birth of the Ultimate Productivity Profile. He said, "I asked them."

In the world of motivating yourself and those around you, a few people make things happen, a few more watch things happen, and the great multitude of people are unaware that anything happened.

I'm quite certain that in your personal and professional life, you are extremely busy. We all have 24 hours every day and manage to fill each of them. Like me, you probably have a "to do" list. Each day is probably scheduled and filled up to overflowing. Most days, some things have to be carried over to tomorrow's list.

So let's imagine you come into the office on a typical Monday morning and look at all the things you need to accomplish before Friday evening. You probably would be questioning whether you or anybody else could get all of these things done in five short work days.

Let's say your boss came in and read over your list with you and the lists of all the colleagues with whom you work. Let's further assume that, after reviewing everyone's calendars, the boss said, "I want everyone to get the entire week's activities concluded by noon Wednesday or else you will suffer the consequences."

You can imagine that a millisecond after the boss exited, there would be wailing, gnashing of teeth, and total outrage regarding the absurd and inhuman demands that your boss had put upon you and your coworkers. It would probably approach the low point of motivation for all concerned. It's not hard to imagine that many people might be formulating their letter of resignation and considering their next career move.

Then imagine the boss returns in the midst of this motivational desert he has just created and announces, "I'm sorry. I failed to mention a small detail when I told you I wanted you to get an entire week's work done by noon Wednesday or you would suffer the consequences. The consequences for not completing your week's work in half the time will be the fact that you will miss the boat. The boat you will miss is a cruise ship that will be leaving that afternoon, taking you, your family, and everyone in this corporation that has completed their week's work on an all-expenses-paid luxury cruise."

As our theoretical boss made his second exit, I'm quite certain we would find a different environment and a significantly altered motivational climate. Remember, nothing changed between what may have been the worst moment in that corporation's history and the best moment in that corporation's history except for the motivation provided and the fact that it was communicated.

The results were not possible without the motivation, but the motivation did not exist without communication.

## CHAPTER ELEVEN

# THE ART OF COMMUNICATING

The aspect of communication is possibly the most important element in productivity. It is the direct link between your motivation and your implementation. I believe it is so important and so lacking in our society that, along with my coauthor Dr. Ray Hull, I wrote an entire book on the subject entitled *The Art of Communication*.

We live in the information age, but it is certainly not the communication age. Many people are laboring under the false assumption that if they simply have more information, more details, and more data, there will be accurate and complete communication. In reality, in the world of communication, the less you can say and still deliver your message the better off you are.

There is a reason why it is against the law in most areas of the country to go into a crowded building and yell, "Fire!" This is only one simple word, and it's not obscene, demeaning, or derogatory in any way, but the reason we are prohibited from yelling, "Fire!" is because that one word instantly and totally communicates the details surrounding a situation that causes people to act immediately and frantically.

Remember, just because you're talking and someone else is listening doesn't mean you are communicating. Communication is the process of getting thoughts, ideas, and concepts from your mind to someone else's. Language, writing, diagrams, and data are all tools to facilitate this transfer, but they can get in the way.

If I told you that it was a really hot day outside, I am expressing this sentiment because—within the databank of my brain—the feeling I have when I'm outside is categorized as hot. When I say those words to you, the databank that is your brain scans your historical perspective and you register a feeling in line with what you have categorized as a hot day. If I live in a tropical area and you live in Alaska, I may communicate to you that it is a hot day, and you may hear what I'm saying to you, but the perspectives are so different that what

I'm saying and what you're hearing are two completely different things.

In addition to the communication breakdown caused by perspective, there is often a communication breakdown created by a transmission problem. All of us have had the experience of talking on a cell phone when you can be having a great conversation one minute, and the next minute the person sounds like Darth Vader speaking Lithuanian.

As you move toward your definition of success through the Art of Productivity, you will be engaging a number of people in your mission. Your challenge will be to maximize communication and avoid miscommunications, partial communication, and false communication.

All of us send and receive communication in different ways. Each of us has a method or system where we excel in communicating, and we all have areas where we are poor communicators.

In the course of my business, I travel extensively each year. This puts me in and out of many hotels across the country and around the world. As a blind person, this can be challenging in that all hotel rooms are set up differently, so in each city I have a new environment to learn.

Each time when I return to my hotel room, I generally call the front desk to see if I have any messages. This usually works well; however, while staying in one particular hotel, the operator answered my inquiry about messages by letting me know that if I had any messages, the light on my phone would be blinking. I let her know that as I am totally blind, their blinking light was not effective for me. Then she showed initiative, if not thought or judgment. From that point on when I received phone messages, instead of activating the blinking light on my phone, she wrote the messages on slips of paper and had the bellman slide them under my door. Just as a totally blind person can't tell whether a light on a phone is blinking, they can't read message slips that have been slid under their door.

She went to a considerable amount of extra effort and energy to communicate with me and elicited the services of the bellman to repeatedly run message slips up to my room, but in the final analysis, we weren't any closer to communicating than we had been before.

As dangerous as it is to not communicate, it can be even more dangerous when you think you have communicated accurately, but the message has either not been received or received in a manner other than you intended.

You've probably heard it said that "There's no such thing as a dumb question." I basically agree with this premise; however, if there were a dumb question, it would be "Do you understand?" Everyone who misunderstands believes they have received the communication clearly and will answer the question in the affirmative even though you have failed to communicate your message and have possibly communicated an opposite message from the one you intended.

The bigger your personal vision of success may be, the more people you will need to communicate with. When I wrote my book entitled *The Ultimate Gift*, the process was the same as the process I am utilizing as I dictate these words to a very talented lady named Dorothy Thompson here in my office. The words somehow come from my brain, I speak them aloud to Dorothy, and she does her spelling and punctuation magic, which creates a book manuscript.

When *The Ultimate Gift* book was turned into *The Ultimate Gift* movie, the process of telling the same story utilized the talents and efforts of hundreds of people. The more people who get involved in a project, the more critical communication becomes.

When it's just me and Dorothy, there is one line of communication—one person receiving and only one source for confirming the communication; however, when you get as large as a movie production company, it necessitates that you create layers of communication. Layers of communication are important, but they are also dangerous. Each time a message is sent and received and then passed on again, there exists the possibility of dilution and distortion.

We all played the game in school where everyone is placed in a circle and a message is whispered into the ear of the first person who, in turn, whispers that message to the second then the third and so on. It is amazing when a message has been sent, filtered, received, and resent by 30 people how distorted and inaccurate it can become.

The simple message that "We rode in my father's Buick to visit my grandmother on summer vacation, and she took us to the zoo,"—30 people removed—can turn into "My grandmother lives at the zoo, and my father drives for Buick on the NASCAR circuit."

This seems like an absurd example of a childhood game gone wrong, but have you ever handed your luggage to an airline employee and clearly told them you were going to Miami and then later had your luggage somehow make its way to Newark? Obviously, school children aren't the only ones who have communication challenges.

The more people who are involved with your team, the more potential you have. You have potential for amazing productivity and, at the same time, you have the potential for unbelievable chaos. As you are building your team to reach your personal success goal, you will need to keep in mind maximizing motivation, communication, and implementation with each team member.

Remember, a lot of people who think they are in management are actually in leadership. You can manage a project, you can manage a task, you can manage money, and you can manage resources, but you can only lead people. People must be motivated, they must send and receive communication, and then they are able to implement the mission that will result in reaching your definition of success. Great managers are those who can attract and retain great people. These leaders understand that everyone on the team is different, and you have to communicate with each of them in different ways.

Let's assume your family is preparing for the possibility of a bad storm. You may collect drinking water, flashlights, transistor radios, and all manner of items calculated to help you should a storm hit your area. Once you get together all of the supplies and tools you need, you have to communicate with each member of the family where they are to go in case of a storm.

Your spouse may be 43 years old and communicating with them is as simple as saying, "If we have a bad storm, let's meet in the basement." Your message has been sent and received, and you have a high likelihood of success; however, if you try the same system and method of communication with four-year-old Amy, you may experience some pitfalls.

Amy may or may not understand exactly what a storm is or how she can tell if one is occurring. She may not be able to determine the difference between a serious storm and a spring rain. She may or may not remember, in a crisis situation, where the basement is, how she should get there, and how to unlatch and open the basement door. Furthermore, if there is any more time elapsed than 20 or 30 minutes from the point you gave Amy your instructions until the storm, she may have forgotten your communications entirely. Amy may be further confused as she tries to differentiate your storm instructions with the fire instructions she received earlier, which told her to get out of the house and meet at the lamppost on the corner. Without accurate, constant, and complete communication, Amy may be in peril because, during a storm, she is standing on the street corner or, during a fire, she is hurrying toward the basement.

Lack of communication can be inconvenient, frustrating, and aggravating, but it can also be costly, dangerous, and devastating.

One of the greatest challenges among leaders who have the task of communicating the elements of a mission with a team striving for success is to determine how much of the big picture should be communicated.

For many years in the corporate world, the thinking has been to only tell people as much as they need to know to perform the immediate task before them. I feel this is ineffective and unproductive, if not completely dangerous.

Communication is the link between motivation and implementation. Often, people cannot be motivated or productively implement their mission if you don't communicate the big picture.

During my college years, I worked on a construction site as a laborer each summer. I was motivated to do a good job and wanted to prove to my coworkers who were older career construction workers that, as a part-time summer worker, I could carry my own weight.

During my first week on the job, the foreman took me to a pile of structural steel and showed me how to attach a crane hook to this structural steel. Then he pointed to a massive crane on the other side of a 30-story building and told me that when the crane operator swung that tall boom over my way, I was to hook the cable to this structural steel so it could be lifted to the top of the building.

The foreman communicated effectively with me, utilizing several good communication techniques. He had given me my instructions verbally, he had demonstrated how to perform the task himself, he had observed me performing the task, he asked me to verbalize back to him what I was going to do, and he answered each of my questions.

So, with confidence that I fully understood my task and the best intentions to perform it promptly and professionally, I stood by and waited for the crane to swing around my way. Several hours passed, and the crane remained engaged constantly lifting materials on the other side of the building. I continued to wait until it was quitting time, and I wasn't sure whether I should stay late or go home, so I continued to stand by—waiting as instructed—for the crane to swing around my way. Finally, it got dark and the crane shut down for the night, so I went home.

The next morning, I resumed my position next to the structural steel, waiting just as I had been told for the crane to swing into position. The waiting went on for a second day and a third.

Finally, on the morning of the fourth day, I was frustrated, confused, and angry. I confronted my foreman and asked, "Do you want me to work here or not?" I went on, "I've been waiting here day after day, trying to do what you told me, and I'm just wasting the company's time and money."

Then the foreman communicated the big picture. He told me that the crane cost many thousands of dollars each day to operate, and I cost virtually nothing in comparison to the crane; therefore, if I had to wait days or even weeks, it wasn't a problem. The only problem would be if the crane swung around my way and I wasn't ready to instantly attach the structural steel so it could be lifted to the top of the building.

My foreman went on to communicate with me that he needed someone trustworthy to be standing by at all times so that we didn't lose one minute of the crane's incredibly valuable and costly time.

As the foreman left me still standing by, waiting for the crane, my entire outlook on the mission and my personal definition of success relating to the task at hand had totally changed. Before I understood the big picture, the prolonged wait for the crane had caused me to lose my motivation and potentially the effectiveness of my implementation.

While the foreman had communicated well and accurately all of the elements of my immediate task, because I didn't understand the big picture his limited communication did not provide a bridge between motivation and implementation.

Communication is not just what to do or how to do it. It includes when to do it, where to do it, who to do it with, and—the often missing element of the Art of Productivity and success—why to do it. If you're going to tell your team what they need to know, they need to understand what success looks like, the total scope of the mission to get from here to there, and the importance of the part they play in it.

## CHAPTER TWELVE

# THE ART OF CUSTOMIZING YOUR MESSAGE

One of the most important pieces of information that you and I own is our name. All of us have had the mortifying experience of being in a professional or social setting when we were introduced to a very important person and, three minutes later, we honestly don't know their name. Obviously, we wanted to know their name, and we recognize it is a critical element of courtesy and respect to call someone by their name;

however, after just being told their name by a mutual friend or contact, we don't know it.

Communication only happens when information is reliably and correctly transferred. Obviously, in the case of our failed introduction, real communication did not take place.

Let's assume that you want to eliminate this problem so, at your next function, everyone is given a name tag. You might, therefore, assume you have permanently resolved the challenge of forgetting someone's name whom you just met.

Although you feel you have a foolproof solution in place, I would submit to you that, for me and millions of other blind or visually impaired people as well as millions of people who are not English readers, you still have not established an effective and reliable line of communication.

In my office building at the Narrative Television Network, we have offices on one floor and studios on the floor below. Adjacent to the studios, I have a private workout room. Several times each day, I leave the office and go downstairs. I stay in communication via a small two-way radio. These radios have 22 channels. While this is a very effective way to communicate, they only work if you're on the right channel. If my office is sending on one channel but I'm receiving on another, there will be absolutely no communication.

No matter how motivated my team is to get hold of me, nor how much they want to implement our mission, the reality is that—for lack of being one channel setting away—our quest for the Art of Productivity is stagnated.

While our radios have 22 settings, human beings come with many more options than that. When we developed the Ultimate Productivity Profile for corporations, investors, and entrepreneurs to determine their own method to achieve the Art of Productivity, we discovered that the widest variety of disconnects come in the field of communication.

Because communication is the most important element of creating success with the team you have around you, and because it is the bridge between motivation and implementation, we've all got to communicate.

All of us lead people and have other people who lead us. If you are an entrepreneur or the CEO of your organization, you may think you are the top dog, but in reality you have a number of people who are leading you. They are called customers. We all answer to someone.

It is important that you understand what your leaders or the marketplace is telling you just as it is critical that you pass along their messages and yours to those whom you lead.

It is impossible to be a great leader without being an excellent communicator. By definition, leaders are people whom other people follow. You cannot become a leader because you declared yourself one or because you decided to be. You have to earn the title and the position of leader.

Earning the right to be a leader first requires you to possess traits that others wish to emulate; but unless you can communicate and demonstrate those traits in a way that others can discern, you are not really a leader.

Our business and personal lives are controlled more and more by the proliferation of technology. You have heard it said that necessity is the mother of invention. It seems to me, in business, that a new invention becomes the mother of necessity.

I have read many books written by and about political, business, and military leaders. In these books, many of their personal and professional letters are reprinted. It is obvious that before the advent of the telephone, everyone got along just fine. But once the telephone was invented, it became a necessity. It's hard to imagine functioning today without a telephone, fax machine, cell phone, and a computer connected to the Internet.

I heard a self-proclaimed business guru recently state that email and instant messaging have revolutionized communications. They have certainly brought about many changes, but they're not all good ones. Because my emails are read to me, I may notice it more than others, but emails are sent so quickly, with very little context, you're often left asking yourself the question, "What does he or she mean by that?"

Remember, if you're the leader within a certain circle of colleagues, your colleagues are very reluctant to blatantly tell you, "I don't know what you're talking about," or "I'm not sure you understand what I mean."

Effective communication requires interaction. An exchange or a dialogue is needed to correct and fine-tune any potential miscommunication. The more avenues you have to communicate through and the more interaction you allow, the better the chances are that communications will, indeed, facilitate the Art of Productivity by building a bridge from motivation to implementation.

Written communications often are left without expression or emphasis so that irony, sarcasm, and the degree of intensity are left out. You may understand what you're typing, but the person on the other end doesn't have a clue.

You could receive the same email from two colleagues that said, "Wow. Yesterday I really had a great flight." One of your colleagues may mean it was the best flight of his life, the service was impeccable, the flight and the landing were smooth, and he reached the gate right on time. Your other colleague sending you the same message may be using sarcasm to express his feelings that the service was nonexistent, the flight and landing resembled a carnival ride, and the delay was measured by a calendar instead of a watch. If, instead of emailing you their thoughts about their flights, you spoke to them on the phone or better yet in person, you would likely quickly determine that one person had the best flight of his life and the other may have had the worst.

Just as there are methods of communication that lend themselves better to different types of interaction, there are people who need specific methods or multiple streams of communication. If your lawyer prepares a 92-page contract and delivers it to you for your signature with a Post-It note that says, "Read and sign," your lawyer has, quite probably, not communicated well—if at all—with you.

A brief phone call or two-paragraph summary would make all the difference in the world; however, you can't replace the contract with a two-paragraph summary. You've got to communicate in the way the message dictates by virtue of its content as well as communicating to the person via the best avenue dictated by their needs and preferences.

As a blind person, I am not able to read this page as you are doing just this moment; however, thanks to recorded books and a high-speed digital player, I complete a full book virtually every day. As the author of more than 30 books, as well as a nationally known speaker and television personality, people contact me regularly wanting to share a book manuscript or screen-play with me.

Over the years, I have noticed that 90 percent of people, even knowing I am blind, simply forward me a printed document as they are seeking my help to get it published or made into a movie or TV show. Approx-imately 10 percent of the people bother to have it recorded or even ask my staff or me what format would be convenient or preferred as a blind person. Given these two approaches, I will leave it to your imagina-tion to determine which type of presentation gets my immediate and full attention.

Sometimes in a difficult or challenging commu-nication environment, it means a great deal when you simply ask those with whom you are communicating if there is a better or preferred delivery method for your message.

I have the privilege of speaking from the platform to literally millions of people, and I have noticed that while my message doesn't dramatically change, the way the audience receives my message and, therefore, the methods I employ shifts dramatically.

I remember speaking to a group of research engi-neers. During a portion of my presentation designed to be particularly humorous, I noticed scattered laughter punctuated by the sound of pens frantically scribbling and notebook pages turning. These high-level academ-ics and mathematicians aren't comfortable determining that content is valid unless they have written it down. They want to see it, read it, and hold it in their hands.

On the other hand, when I talked to a group of sales people or media people, they are distracted if not totally put off if my presentation is not delivered in a way that it is totally verbal.

With one group, I am communicating with logic, reason, and facts. With another group, I am communicating the same message with humor, emotion, and visualization. Both methods are valid, but they are never interchangeable.

There are a few communications in your personal and professional life in which the best method is probably obvious. If someone is taking a phone message for you, it is probably best that they at least get the name and number in writing; however, a message that says, "Fred called concerning his order. 555-2321" can mean a myriad of things that can only be clarified when the verbal exchange that took place when Fred called is communicated.

Fred may be concerned about his order in that he is so excited to receive your product and service that he wants to be sure he can order more. On the other hand, Fred may have been violently yelling at your receptionist as he communicated his concern that if the order didn't get there by tomorrow he was canceling.

If you don't know which environment you're getting ready to step into, you may be going into battle without any weapons. If you haven't already communicated with your receptionist that you want to be alerted to the different situations, you need to let them know you expect and welcome their full understanding of the call.

Two executives might be returning from lunch and both receive a message from their spouse. "Just called to see what was going on." Executive A's spouse just had an extra moment between appointments and wanted to call and see how everything was going today. Executive B's spouse is calling because Executive B was supposed to meet the spouse for lunch and is 45 minutes late. This would be impossible to determine from a scribbled phone message but almost impossible to miss in a verbal exchange.

Written instructions, as well as verbal ones, always make sense to the person delivering them. Everything makes sense to me in my mind. My challenge in life is to get that message of clarity that I have in my mind into a book, a newspaper column, a speech, or a movie.

As important as the day-in, day-out routine communications are, it is even more critical that the motivation you feel inside of you is accurately communicated to your entire team. There is a big difference between what you want someone to do and what you want done as I described earlier. Standing around waiting for a crane may be what you want someone to do, while having a responsible person on call to maximize the efficiency of a valuable asset like a crane is what you want done.

The more elements of the big picture you can communicate to everyone on your team, the better your chances of success. No matter how much you are motivated and how badly you wish to implement, unless you have accurate communications with everyone around you, you are simply all dressed up with nowhere to go.

## CHAPTER THIRTEEN

# THE ART OF IMPLEMENTATION

Implementation is one of the most misunderstood elements of the Art of Productivity. Many people who are not achieving their personal definition of success believe that implementation means starting. As you and I have discovered, implementation is part of a seamless process that begins with defining your own success, establishing a mission, evaluating your passion, creating motivation, and communicating all of these elements in a way that will make success inevitable.

Many people feel, when they watch the 100-meter dash in the Olympics, that implementation means settling into the starting blocks and waiting for the starter's gun to sound. In reality, that 100-meter dash began for those Olympians years before with dreams, planning, training, qualifying, and, finally, the opportunity to have the entire process culminate in one ten-second dash.

Proper implementation does not come naturally to human beings. There are those among us who want to engage their fight or flight instinct and begin a lifelong quest as a knee-jerk reaction to some random stimulus. On the other hand, there are those poor souls who have fallen victim to the analysis paralysis, and they are not going to leave their house until all the lights are green.

General George Patton is among my favorite historical figures because he certainly knew how to plan, prepare, handle logistics, and analyze all factors; but he also knew how to light the fuse and implement. General Patton said, "A good plan violently executed today is better than a perfect plan next week."

There is a great newspaperman in my hometown who called me a number of years ago after reading my books. He complimented me on my writing and asked if I had ever written a column. I told him I had not even considered it, and he asked me to fax him 400 to 500 words. About 10 to 15 minutes later, I sent the fax and never thought any more about it.

He ran the column the following week and called me and said the words that turned me into a newspaper, magazine, and online columnist around the world: "Just do that every week."

In the beginning, I would worry and fret about each week's column until he gave me another piece of great advice. "This is a newspaper. We don't need it perfect. We need it Thursday." That was almost 1,000 columns ago, and writing my weekly *Winners' Wisdom* column has become an automatic, routine part of my life.

There are millions of people around the world who have read my columns, and the first edition of them has been released as a book entitled *Wisdom for Winners*, and there is a follow-up book, *Wisdom for Winners Two*, with more in the works. This all became possible when I understood the proper implementation principles relating to my definition of success as a weekly columnist.

Perfection is something we should strive for, and it should motivate us to move ahead. Unfortunately for too many people, perfection becomes an unachievable ideal that creates an environment where they simply never begin.

As you and I discovered earlier, every time you take an airplane flight you are off course the vast majority of the time, and the pilots would tell you that the conditions are never totally perfect. The reason we have an airline industry and the ability to travel anywhere in the world in hours instead of months is because pioneers dreamed of a system and created an industry that recognizes that, within the bounds of safety, there are any number of conditions that will allow for a perfectly routine flight, and we're all off course from time to time. The key to implementation is to take off and adjust.

Those who overcome the temptation to fall victim to analysis paralysis can often fall into the ready, fire, aim trap. This life you and I are living right now is not a practice game. It is our own Super Bowl, World Series, and Olympics all rolled up into one powerful, passionate process. While we don't want to sit around contemplating the conditions and analyzing all elements until we lose the window of opportunity, we also don't want to minimize our potential by not going through the valid steps of the Art of Productivity.

Anything worth the investment of our time, effort, and energy is worth planning and utilizing motivation and communication principles as we prepare to implement.

If you went to a local grocery store and noticed people at the checkout counter, you would discover that the majority of people who have more than one or two items came to the grocery store with a shopping list. They don't want to waste the time, effort, and energy it took to do their grocery shopping by forgetting something they really need and then being forced to return to the store.

I remember as a child working on some carpentry project with my grandfather. He explained to me the wisdom of measuring twice and cutting once. His words have stayed with me for several decades. "If you don't have time to do it right, when are you going to have time to do it over?"

The old adage that you must plan your work and work your plan is really true. We all have limited time, energy, creativity, and resources. If you're going to reach your own destiny through your personal definition of success, you've got to utilize everything you've been given by employing the Art of Productivity.

Rarely will you achieve more than you have planned, and you will never achieve all you can unless you have created your Art of Productivity blueprint. There are many ways to implement that take into account your and your team's individual characteristics, but all implementation styles have certain success principles in place that relate to the Art of Productivity.

As I am dictating these words to you, I am seated in an office within the Narrative Television Network, which is the company I founded and run. Several times during the process of dictating this chapter, I will be interrupted by a phone call or a person here in the office with a quick question. This doesn't bother me as I have never been a temperamental writer. I know authors who literally have to move into a mountain cabin and be surrounded with total silence before they can write. There are great writers who get up early in the morning and write a few pages each day. There are other writers who start sometime after the world has gone to bed and write late into the night or until dawn. There are writers who type into a computer. Others still use a manual typewriter. And I even know extremely successful authors who write longhand on a yellow pad.

All of these styles can succeed and do succeed for writers who establish their own personal definition of success, create their own writing mission, pursue the works they publish with a passion, create their own motivation, communicate it to everyone around them, and—within a system that works for them—they implement.

If you desire to be a published author but only want to work at your craft for a half an hour every New Year's Eve, I submit to you this would not work. If you're not willing to learn the most rudimentary elements of spelling, grammar, and punctuation, you don't have a chance. And, finally, if you don't learn the basics of the publishing industry and work within those broad expectations that have been established, you're probably never going to be the guest of honor at your own book signing. On the other hand, in most endeavors there are few rules that will confine you and many ways to implement your mission that will result in you reaching your personal definition of success.

When I started the Narrative Television Network, which makes movies, television, and educational programs accessible for the 13 million blind and visually impaired Americans and millions more around the world, I realized that nothing exactly like NTN had ever been done before. Even though I knew we were going to be breaking some new ground, I also realized that there were certain basic rules and expectations within the broadcast and cable industry that needed to guide our implementation.

The industry utilizes certain electronic signals, bandwidth, tape formats, and other technical specifications that must be adhered to. Television programs have to fall within standard one-hour or half-hour slots, and commercials need to conform to the style, timing, and expectations of the advertising industry; however, once you've covered the basics, you still have some freedom to implement outside of the box.

After we pulled together a little bit of programming and a few broadcast and cable affiliates across the country, I realized if we were ever going to make any money, we were going to have to sell some advertising and fill up our commercial slots. We located a book that had a list of the top 100 advertisers in America. I felt these would be good prospects, because I have a theory on selling: If you're going to sell, sell to people who buy.

A lot of entrepreneurs and sales people waste precious time and potential by repeatedly beating a dead horse. So, armed with my list of 100 prospects, I began calling them all each day. I have had people sit in my audiences at conventions and arena events who later have challenged me by emphatically stating, "You can't call 100 people every day." Well, I actually enjoy bursting their bubble when I tell them, "Yes, you can. It takes about six-and-one-half hours. I know this because I did it for many months."

The reality is that when you cold call the head of advertising at some of the largest corporations in the world, they won't all talk to you the first day, or the first week, or even the first month. You've got to be willing to break them in or, in my case, maybe wear them down.

So day after day after day, I would call each of the 100 prospects I had established, placing a checkmark by their name after the call. I remember well the day that one flustered advertising executive got on the phone with me and said, "Mr. Stovall, I don't know who you are, but do you realize that you have phoned my office 57 days in a row?"

I chuckled and replied, "Yes, sir. I'm well aware of that, because your name is right here in my notebook that lists my 100 prospects that I call each day. And if you don't hear my story today, I'll be calling you tomorrow and the next day and the day after that."

Please understand, I am not an annoying, pushy sales person. I am simply someone who established a personal goal, forged a mission, and generated passion and motivation that I communicated to my team and prospects as I implemented through my sales calls.

Now, you're probably thinking, "I wouldn't have done it that way." I wouldn't disagree with you and, if I had it to do over again, I probably wouldn't do it that way again either; however, implementing in that fashion generated enough success for the Narrative Television Network to become a viable and growing television network.

While you and I might not do it that way again, the fact of the matter is that if we implement it in another way, we still would have to get our story and opportunity in front of the right people who would help us succeed through the Art of Productivity.

You should never be married to methods, but you must be unwavering when it comes to your mission toward your personal success. Unfortunately, if you don't examine yourself thoroughly and honestly, you will find it very difficult to implement the Art of Productivity on your way to success. We all have human weaknesses and, too often, take the course of least resistance.

Coach Wooden told me that most players want to practice the elements of basketball where they already excel. Players want to practice the three-point shot or dunking the basketball, when, in reality, free throws and defense are what win championships.

When you consider implementing the Art of Productivity relating to your personal definition of success, you've got to know yourself and be willing to do the things that mediocre people won't do, which are the same things you won't do unless you utilize the Art of Productivity through motivation, communication, and implementation.

## CHAPTER FOURTEEN

# THE ART OF PULLING THE TRIGGER

No matter how well you have established your personal definition of success, crafted your mission, infused passion into your goal, and regardless of how well you are motivated and communicate all elements of the Art of Productivity, unless you implement, all is lost. More people fail to start than fail to succeed. There is no shame in striking out while offering your best efforts and being willing to get up to the plate again. The shame comes in never having tried.

Timid souls will tell you, "If you set a goal and pursue it with passion, you could fail and be disappointed." The boldest among us would say, "If you try and try again, you will eventually succeed. If you don't try, you will inevitably and absolutely fail."

As a platform speaker, I have the privilege of going to many wonderful events and meeting outstanding human beings. As I first began studying the Art of Productivity and the elements that make up the Ultimate Productivity Profile and assessment, I had just returned from speaking at the tournament banquet for the PGA Championship where Tiger Woods won his 13th major championship and fourth PGA title. Tiger Woods may be the best known example in his generation of someone who implements through the Art of Productivity.

He makes everything seem as if it is easy for him to implement. I can assure you, the performance you see in major championships around the world is the result of many hours of preparation and planning.

One particular shot during the final round of the championship required Tiger Woods to hit an exacting shot over 200 yards and stop the ball within a few feet on a very slick and sun baked green. Most of the 200 yards the shot required Tiger to carry were over water. This strikes fear in most average golfers, but for Tiger Woods, implementing the shot is mere routine. He takes the same number of practice swings, approaches the ball in the same way, and executes the swing as he has done it thousands of times.

Success is never easy, and just because you have established your own definition of success and followed the steps of the Art of Productivity through motivation, communication, and implementation, never assume it won't take a maximum effort from you. While I can assure you that there is a great cost in time, effort, and energy to succeed, I can further assure you that the cost of failure is even higher.

It is important that you systematize the implementation of your success. You want to eliminate as many variables as possible and make productive implementation a part of your routine.

Speaking in front of an audience is recognized by most psychologists and those who study human thought to be among the most frightening and fearful of experiences. When people ask me how I speak to millions of people without seeming to be intimidated, the answer is quite simple. It becomes routine. Any great performance, be it on stage, on the golf course, or in your pursuit of your personal goal through the Art of Productivity, is a product of routine.

The human mind literally cannot tell the difference between reality and something vividly imagined. This is why you experience the physiological signs of fright while watching a horror movie. You know it's only a movie, but your respiration will quicken and your pulse will increase. The more times you watch the same movie, the less of a physical reaction you will experience until, finally, it becomes so routine that you have no physical reaction at all.

If you are pursuing any worthwhile goal, it will be difficult. The difficulty is multiplied when you add to it the stress or pressure of pursuing something you are so passionate about. This can be eliminated when you systematize your implementation.

It is not as important what system you use as it is important that you establish a system. Tiger Woods' routine works for him. Other successful golfers have their own routine that works well for them. The details are not important; however, if Tiger Woods tried to use another golfer's pre-shot routine, it would throw off his rhythm and balance, and he would begin to think and evaluate instead of simply implementing.

People who work in high-stress, high-impact jobs such as firefighters, police officers, and military personnel are trained to react without thinking. If, every time a firefighter was called upon to perform a rescue in a burning building, he stopped and considered all the danger involved for himself and everyone around him, he would be so stagnated in his thought process he could not implement.

I recommend that you take the long-term goal you have turned into a mission and reduce it to daily activities. You simply have to determine what you would need to do today in order to reach your five-year or ten-year goal.

Life and success come down to implementing on a day-by-day basis. Make a list of the things that have to be done today if you're going to get one day closer to your personal definition of success today. Then, as you look at the list of tasks that must be completed, there will generally be one or two you wish you didn't have to do. I suggest you do these first.

As the legendary Coach John Wooden told us, people want to practice the things they like and need to practice the things they don't. I suggest that when we are passionate and motivated we should practice our defense and free-throws so that at the end of the day we can do the fun things like shooting the three-point shots and dunking the basketball.

Most sales people don't like cold calls, so they habitually dread these calls and put them off until late in the day. This creates a situation where the negative emotion attached to the cold calls permeates all activities, and if there are any interruptions or unexpected obligations, the cold calls aren't even made, and the sales person is one day further from success.

Any worthwhile goal requires implementation of tasks we don't like. If it was fun and easy, everybody would do it, and they would all already be successful. Set the highest hurdles up first so that once you clear them it's downhill for the rest of the day.

There are as many ways to implement a task as there are people. I am an early riser and enjoy doing my critical and strategic thinking between 4:00 and 5:00 a.m. I realize, in your mind, this puts me in the category of a minority or possibly a category of insanity, but this has always worked well for me. On the other hand, I know people who do their best thinking and strategizing long after midnight. I know people who must work in absolute silence and others who require blaring music. Some people like to complete one task and then go to the next in a linear fashion while others like to trade off a few minutes of each activity throughout the day. There are people who only feel competent and professional when they are formally dressed for success and others who prefer to work from home in their bathrobe. It is important that you find your power groove that works for you when you are implementing.

We all have coaches and mentors who lead us and guide us. They are important, but remember—observe what they do and how they do it. What they do is universal. How they do it is personal and individual.

If you wanted to be a pitcher in the Major Leagues, it would be important for you to have coaches and mentors. Warren Spahn is recognized as having one of the greatest Major League careers of any pitcher who ever stood atop the mound. I had the privilege of meeting him on a cross-country flight and learned many lessons about success and productivity during our time together. He later became a coach and helped many young ball players reach their potential. Warren Spahn had great rhythm, timing, and a tremendous release when he threw the ball. He was also a left-handed pitcher. If you are right-handed, you can learn from Warren Spahn rhythm, timing, and release, but you should not start throwing the ball left-handed if you are naturally a right-handed person. You've got to use the universal principles that work for everyone but implement them on a personal basis customized for you.

One of the things that concerns me about our school system today is the fact that everyone is expected to implement in the same way. There was actually a time in the not-too-distant past when all students in public schools being taught penmanship were required to write with their right hand. This seems absurd to us now because we know there are people who are naturally left-handed; so the thought of forcing them to implement in a less-productive way seems ridiculous. Although we have overcome that hurdle, there are still many examples of forced universal implementation in our educational system.

We all recognize those who succeed in life. They are generally creative, expansive, outgoing people who think and implement outside the box. They are known for coming up with new and better ways to do things. This makes them productive and, in our society, being productive or implementing the Art of Productivity spells success. While we recognize this after the fact, rarely do we allow people to explore their own individual strengths while they are being educated and trained.

There are certain tasks that require everyone to perform the same way. Pilots and copilots have a standard routine as they go through the flight checklist. There is no room for creativity or individuality in the process; however, I am appalled when I see educators and trainers who think all sales people, writers, artists, and entrepreneurs should be cookie-cutters of one another.

There are more millionaires alive and succeeding in the world today than ever before. Despite the gloom and doom you may read in the media regarding economic conditions, the facts are that the rate of new millionaires is actually accelerating. The rich are, indeed, getting richer. People are succeeding faster than they ever did before.

You and I learned earlier that money does not equal success in and of itself, but it is probably the easiest way to keep score and, therefore, compare and contrast the way to best implement your Art of Productivity.

Right after World War II, if you had surveyed average people on the street and asked them how most millionaires got to be millionaires, the majority would have told you that most wealthy people inherited their money. That wasn't the case then and is even less the case today. Fully 90 percent of the almost 10 million millionaires in the United States today are first-generation. They earned, saved, and invested their way to becoming a millionaire. While there are certain universal principles that all financially successful people have employed, there are as many ways to become a millionaire as there are millionaires.

As a blind person myself, I had a tremendous advantage in becoming a millionaire. It was readily apparent to me and anyone around me that I could not perform normal tasks in the standard way; therefore, I was forced to find alternative ways to reach my goals that suited me the best. I was forced out of the mold that has been established for most of us to follow.

You are going to have to exercise your right to choose, make a quality decision, and change your life by making a conscious decision to find and utilize your unique strengths and talents as you implement the Art of Productivity on your way to your own personal success.

While the whole world is trying to cram us all into a one-size-fits-all societal norm for success, the truth remains that your success is a personal destination known only to you. It can only be reached by undergoing an individualized mission for which you were designed.

Power and passion are the natural results of undertaking a mission toward your personal success. While the whole world may want to force us onto a crowded train leaving at a scheduled time toward a pre-determined destination, the universe we live in is full of unique and magical wonders.

You have a personal destiny, a customized vehicle designed to get you from here to there, and more than enough fuel for the journey. If you will listen to and follow those who have been to their own unique mountaintops instead of following the herd onto the crowded train, you will live a life unknown and unimaginable to the masses of humanity.

You won't succeed because you're better than anyone else. You'll succeed because success is defined by you, and there is no one ready, willing, or able to fill your unique role better than you.

## CHAPTER FIFTEEN

# THE ART OF TAKING ACTION

After interacting with hundreds of corporations and many thousands of people through my books, columns, and speeches, I have come to the conclusion that there is a basic disconnect between most people who say they have goals and their reality.

I developed the Ultimate Productivity Profile (www.UltimateProductivity.com) to help corporations, entrepreneurs, and investors find the most productive path to their personal definition of success through motivation, communication, and implementation. You and your colleagues can take the Ultimate Productivity

Profile and get your own free assessment by logging on to the site mentioned above and using your access code 586404. I believe you have those tools in your possession now, or at least you have the capacity to develop your customized tools for the Art of Productivity; but without action, it's all just a fairy tale. If you don't act upon the things you have learned in these pages, your current once-upon-a-time will not end up in your living happily ever after.

I hate to be the one to have to tell you, but life is not fair. It is great, grand, and wonderful, but not fair. In this life, you will not always get what you want, need, earn, or deserve, but you will, indeed, get what you expect.

If you will keep your personal definition of success in the forefront of your mind as you move into your future by pursuing your mission with passion, your tomorrows will be different from your today.

Unfortunately, many people try to move into their future while dragging their past along with them. This simply doesn't work. Your past has defined who you are today. The action you will take today will define who you will be in the future, unless you fail to release your past.

One of my favorite animals to study is the spider monkey. Spider monkeys are small primates that have many characteristics like human beings. Spider monkeys live in the tallest trees in the rain forest of the Amazon basin in South America.

For many years, explorers tried to capture the spider monkeys. First, they tried to capture these little primates in giant nets suspended from the trees. But the spider monkeys were too small and too fast, so they could slip through and around the nets and scurry to safety. Next, the explorers tried to capture the spider monkeys with dart guns containing tranquilizers; however, there were too many leaves and branches between the explorers and the treetops where the spider monkeys dwell.

The explorers were frustrated in every attempt to capture the spider monkeys until one of the natives showed them the secret. And now, I'm going to share that secret with you.

The way you capture a spider monkey is to put one peanut inside of a clear glass bottle. You have now constructed the perfect spider monkey trap. You then place the bottle containing the peanut at the base of a tree, and you leave the area.

While you're gone, the spider monkey will look far down the tree and see that peanut in the bottle. He will eventually climb down the tree and put his little hand in the bottle and grab the peanut. His clinched fist holding the peanut is too large to get out of the bottle, so—presto! You have captured a spider monkey.

You can return an hour, a day, or even a week later, and that little spider monkey will be standing there holding on to that peanut inside the bottle that he really didn't want in the first place and he can't eat anyway. You can place a whole bag of peanuts on the ground next to the spider monkey, but he'll continue to stand there, clutching the one lone peanut that isn't doing him a bit of good. You can put bananas all around him on the ground, but he will continue to stand there holding that useless peanut.

He may eventually starve to death if you don't help him out of his self-imposed trap. You can even have other spider monkeys playing all around him, but the trapped spider monkey will stand there all alone clutching one useless peanut that is destroying his future.

You can take away his freedom, or you can take away his very life, but our little spider monkey will simply not be willing to let go of one worthless peanut to gain everything in the world that matters to him.

After conducting exhaustive research myself into the behavior of spider monkeys—I probably shouldn't call it exhaustive research, but I have read two books on the subject—I have come to the inescapable conclusion that spider monkeys are stupid. But lest I be too critical of these poor little primates and before you and I can laugh at their behavior, we need to ask ourselves one haunting question: What is it in your life that you are holding on to that is keeping you from everything you ever wanted?

If you're going to have personal success, you have got to let go of all those images of past failures. If you're going to have peace, happiness, and joy, you have got to let go of resentment and experience forgiveness. And while you're forgiving people, don't forget the most important person you need to forgive. Please forgive yourself.

Remember, all of that garbage you're carrying around inside of you defines who you used to be in the past. Your personal definition of success is a vision you can carry with you into the future as you pursue your mission with the passion that will lead you to your destiny.

You are a unique person with a special, customized, tailor-made destiny. You already have all of the tools necessary to get from here to there in the form of your own motivation, communication, and implementation. My greatest desire for you is that you see yourself in that way and take action. If not now, when? And if not you, who?

I am looking forward to your success, and once you capture the vision of your future which contains your personal definition of success, you'll never be the same again.

# ABOUT JIM STOVALL

In spite of blindness, Jim Stovall has been a National Olympic weightlifting champion, a successful investment broker, the president of the Emmy Award-winning Narrative Television Network, and a highly sought-after professional speaker. He is the author of 30 books, including the bestseller, *The Ultimate Gift,* which is now a major motion picture from 20th Century Fox starring James Garner and Abigail Breslin. Five of his other novels have also been made into major motion pictures.

Steve Forbes, president and CEO of *Forbes* magazine, says, "Jim Stovall is one of the most extraordinary men of our era."

For his work in making television accessible to our nation's 13 million blind and visually impaired people, The President's Committee on Equal Opportunity selected Jim Stovall as the Entrepreneur of the Year. Jim Stovall has been featured in *The Wall Street Journal*, *Forbes* magazine, *USA Today*, and has been seen on *Good Morning America, CNN,* and *CBS Evening News*. He was also chosen as the International Humanitarian of the Year, joining Jimmy Carter, Nancy Reagan, and Mother Teresa as recipients of this honor.

Jim Stovall can be reached at 918-627-1000 or Jim@JimStovall.com.

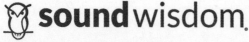